RAISING A JOYFUL FAMILY

THE CHRISTIAN READER BOOK ON
RAISING A JOYFUL FAMILY

Edited by Jeanne Hunt

1817

HARPER & ROW, PUBLISHERS, SAN FRANCISCO
Cambridge, Hagerstown, New York, Philadelphia
London, Mexico City, São Paulo, Sydney

FIRST EDITION

Library of Congress Cataloging in Publication Data

Main entry under title:

THE CHRISTIAN READER BOOK ON RAISING A JOYFUL FAMILY.

    1. Family—Religious life—Addresses, essays, lectures. I. Hunt, Jeanne. II. Christian reader. III. Title: Raising a joyful family.
BV4526.2.C45 1983   248.8'4   82-48423
ISBN 0-06-061387-4

---

83 84 85 86 87 10 9 8 7 6 5 4 3 2 1

COPYRIGHT ACKNOWLEDGMENTS

Contents

Guidelines to Happy Families by Gladys M. Hunt

If someone could come up with ten easy steps to insure a happy family, he would have a highly marketable product. But happiness is not for sale. Alas, the basic ingredient of the formula involves *being*, personal *being*. Not a formula out there to apply, but a personal integrity lived out in full view of all the family members.

It begins with the mother and father. A child has an uncanny way of perceiving the dynamics of relationship between the mother and the father. No matter how polite and cool the tone of voice, if disrespect, anger, manipulation, or deceit play a part in the interpersonal transactions of mother and father, you have undercut the best of formulas or principles.

People play such strange games with each other if they aren't working at being whole (holy) and honest in their relationships. That's why it is not enough to say that a happy family begins with a Christian mother and father. One needs to ask: What kind of a Christian mother and father? The kind that makes a public commitment by joining the church, and then never opens the Bible except in church? The kind that frets and worries as if God didn't exist? The kind that grabs at worldly achievements to fill empty places inside? The kind that uses Scripture verses as a club to enforce personal opinions, but does not let the whole of the Word of God enter the life to cleanse and to instruct?

I know of a mother and father, conspicuous in Christian activity, whose communication at home has a twisted quality to it that makes it difficult for their children to survive in the environment. Yet with a developed skill for manipulation, the mother writes letters to her children from God and posts them on their doors. Whatever she says is synonymous with what God says—when it suits her purposes.

Another set of parents are great on making rules and issuing edicts, but their inconsistency in following up on the rules makes them a mockery to be exploited by the children. Oh, they believe things—true things—but with roller-coaster constancy.

The first ingredient for a happy family is a well-put-together mother and father. They will not be perfect, but they are working at evicting the dragons from their souls and have established a loving relationship together that gives their children a sense of security. Within the circle of home there is *safety, safety* because there is genuine love, open communication, and a way of handling conflict that is well-defined and acceptable.

This is important to stress at the outset because principles are not applied in isolation. It's a package deal. Why? Because we are whole people. We can't give a dose of medicine to the body and forget the emotions. Nor can we instruct the mind and forget the spirit. God wants us to be whole people who are holy. Happiness grows out of that. There is no substitute for integrity in the inner person!

Having said that, here are ten guidelines for happy family life.

Communication. Words alone don't spell communication. A buffoon for a father may score high in word output, but be totally unknown as a real person to his children. Most mothers talk a lot, but that doesn't mean communication takes place.

Communication implies a message given and received. Love needs to be communicated in words and in deeds. I am simply amazed at the university students who aren't sure they are loved by their parents. The only gauge they have for checking is *things.* Verbal expression (I love you. You're a neat person.) and physical expression (spontaneous hugs and kisses) are missing. And so are the small ways of going out of the way to express appreciation for another's personhood.

Ideas need to be communicated. People who live together should know how the other person feels inside and how he thinks. What are his views about what makes life meaningful? It should be safe to be known in this household. Expression of what is deep and important to a person can only take place in a safe environment. The parents take the lead and give the example in a willingness to be known, to be vulnerable.

Communication also means that any subject is open for discussion. I do not believe this gives license to vulgarity, for within the love of this home the children learn what is appropriate to discuss and what is idle curiosity. Answers that are honestly sought are different from smart-aleck inquiries into what is inappropriate. However, too many families suffer from shocked silence over what ought to be discussed and fit into a thoroughly consistent view of God and the world. If parents were discussing the realities of life, their children would understand better how the ten commandments are rules for our happiness, rather than negative ideas to spoil our fun.

Expect good communication; communicate yourself.

Consistency. Thou art a gem! No single principle has so far-reaching an effect. Consistency helps make the world safe. Consistency in values. In discipline. In religious faith. In love. In faithfulness. In understanding.

We live in a feeling-oriented world that fights against consistency. Many people chase after fads in religion, suffer disappointment, lapse into inactivity and then jump on the next wagon that makes them feel good. And then wonder why their children aren't interested in God.

Or the parents who insist on the evils of marijuana (rightfully) but who gossip or lie shamelessly in front of their children. Every parent needs to ask, am I consistent in all areas of my life?

Expect consistency; be consistent.

Presence. Not things. Long business hours, working mothers, traveling fathers. How do you make up for not being there? Bring a present, hand him a check, buy her a new dress. Children respond to absence without complaint while they are young. The tragedy is that they complain when it is too late.

Presence says, "I care. We need to be together." It may mean rejection of a promotion, a refusal to climb the corporate ladder. Ideally, however, presence has quality, not just quantity.

Be present yourself; expect your family to be there, too.

Acceptance. Acceptance is a climate, not a duty performed. Like nourishment that makes the spirit strong, acceptance creates an environment of love and forgiveness. Acceptance is rooted in the heart of God. We accept others because we feel accepted by him. The love of God allows each of us to be unique, not forced into the mold of a brother or sister. It allows us to become vulnerable by loving others.

11

Acceptance does not mean tolerating wrong. True love always desires another's highest good. But the environment of acceptance makes growth and change possible.

Parents create environments in which people learn how to love and forgive one another.

Respect. Respect grows out of acceptance. Respect says you are valuable because you are a person God made. Children are people—people who need respect.

Having just gotten off the yellow school bus one day, our five-year-old came into the house, slammed the back door and leaned against it in relief. "Well," he said, "I sure like that bus driver. He treats me like I'm a people." After having been herded, shouted at, threatened with the mob of little persons who rode the bus, he had at last been treated with dignity! We laughed at his five-year-old wisdom. Since then, "treating me like I'm a people" is part of our household vocabulary.

Probably every mother in the world has at some time heard her child speak to another with her tone of voice and winced with the pain of recognizing her own words. How often some look back with resentment on the words or treatment of their own parents that wounded them, and yet reproduce the identical statement or attitudes toward their own offspring.

This is to say that parents are models in learning respect. Children should see mother treating father with respect, and father openly demonstrating respect for mother. If we treat children respectfully, they will return the same kind of treatment. We have the right to insist upon it, and to expect it to flow across to all family members.

Priorities. Learn to separate the trivial from the crucial. Unless you can see what is really important you will not teach your children what is valuable.

Recently I heard a father recount a discussion in which he had tangled with his son over wearing blue jeans to church. It was difficult for the father, brought up with the concept of a Sunday suit and Sunday shoes, to imagine why his son would even want to wear jeans to church. He could have made it an issue of submission to authority, but he decided not to. It seemed pharisaical to him to be more concerned about outward appearance. The son had the dress preference of his peers, but an open heart to God. The father

12

judged the openness to God of greater value than the wearing of jeans.

You may disagree with the specifics of this illustration, but I think the father had an eye for separating the crucial from the trivial. Far too often families fuss over trivia and neglect the issues that make for integrity of character, compassionate understanding, and simple godliness.

Some issues may not seem like trivia. They need to be weighed in terms of eternity. The decision about the relative importance of working all summer ("You have a job when other kids don't") or taking a month off for Christian training puts priorities in another ball park. What are your long-range goals? What, exactly, do you want to teach your child by the priorities chosen? How do you demonstrate your own willingness to trust God?

Let your priorities demonstrate what you think is valuable.

Submission to authority. The most convincing evidence of the reality of Christian faith for a child is to see both father and mother living under the Lordship of Jesus Christ. We are under authority. Our children need to understand that the Word of God vitally concerns our living patterns. They must see its truths cut into our lives and change us. The family unit comes under the authority of God.

You cannot give your children a more valuable treasure than an adequate view of God. I don't mean that you can package all of God up and deliver it to your children, but what they believe about God will condition all of their life choices. What is true about him is found in the Scripture and must be handled with carefulness and integrity. The warped, inadequate, distorted view of God is reflected in stunted, twisted lives.

Children project their experience with their parents onto God. The Fatherhood of God has a distorted image to a child who doesn't have a good view of an earthly father. Children need to have teaching underscored with living.

The moral code of the family will come from the Scripture, not be imposed on to its teaching. The family comes under all of God's authority on every point. If children do not observe their parents obeying God, obedience to any authority is weakened. Parents derive their authority from God, who says, "Children, obey your parents in the Lord, for this is right." The whole chain of authority

13

relationships is set up under God in the home and will condition the child's ability to live in relationship with others in society and to obey God.

Family teaching is, therefore, crucial. You cannot leave to any school or church the instruction which is parental responsibility. Yet statistics show that only ten percent of Christian families have any kind of family Bible reading or instruction. To complain that there isn't time takes us back to the necessity of priority. Will we be silent in the face of the barrage of influences that hit our children every day?

Live under authority; expect your children to do so.

Discipline. Disciples are the goal of discipline. No discipline is pleasant at the time, but rather uncomfortable. Yet afterwards it yields peaceable fruits of righteousness in the lives of those who have been exercised by it (Hebrews 12).

The punishment should fit the crime. Don't make the discipline for lying or cheating the same as for spilling milk. Don't make idle threats. Consistent discipline affords genuine security to children who generally push parents as far as they can. If "no" means "no," then say it only once. Otherwise the child will never know when you will mean it, and if he knows how to push you at five years, he'll be three times better at it at 15.

Always separate the deed from the child. We love the child so much we *must* discipline. Never say, "You are a bad, bad girl." The deed is wrong, but the child is not worthless. Give expectation of growth, and don't remember every past wrong. Demonstrate that you know what forgiveness is.

Your ability to discern between what is trivial and what is crucial will keep you from making too many rules and keeping the boundaries too narrow. One of the goals of discipline is to encourage the ability to make yourself do what is right whether you feel it or not.

Be a disciple; encourage discipleship in your children.

Responsibility. Privilege and responsibility go together. Develop a feel for *our* family and *our* home where each takes a share of responsibility and concern for others and the place we live.

For this reason, I think monetary allowances should be given apart from duties done. We participate in household responsibilities and care for each other simply because we belong to this family and to this household. We are not paid to be responsible.

14

Make the guidelines clear. Have a well-understood operating procedure. And be generous with praise. Expect a lot; get a lot.

Adventure. Be a together-family. Eat together. Read together. Plan adventures together, even when it may not be the first choice of every family member. Be prepared to vary your adventures and learn from each other. ●

The Home Against the World by Letha Scanzoni

"**I** tremble to see my children grow up in this godless world," says one of today's mothers. "You try to bring them up so they'll accept Christ as Savior. You do all you can to teach them the Bible. Yet you're still not sure how they'll turn out."

"These are dark days," murmurs a grandmother. "Things get worse and worse. I pity young families who still have their children to raise."

You don't have to go far to hear statements like these. They are voiced increasingly, and they present a pessimistic picture.

But they don't have to! There *is* hope for our young people. After all, has any period of history been an easy age to bring up children for Christ? There is no good reason why we cannot take God at his word and train up a child in the way he should go, being assured that God keeps promises and our child will not depart from that way in later life.

The word "train" is the key. Christians sometimes limit it to mean participation in religious exercises (Sunday school and church attendance, grace at meals, family devotions, and the like). But the Bible's instruction encompasses far more. Training is more than telling. It's helping our children to think through spiritual matters for themselves. It's showing our youngsters how Jesus Christ can relate to every part of their lives.

Training means helping our children to form attitudes and to develop values and goals around which their lives will be built. It means guidance which is loving and discipline that instructs. It means helping our children to find answers to the puzzling problems they confront at each stage of life. Training should be going on all the time—all day long.

Nothing influences the young child more than his home life. His

16

little world revolves around his parents. Yet too often we fail to seize the opportunity, to "redeem the time" in our own families. There are at least three reasons why this is so.

(1) Busyness. Caught up in the activism which too many churches take to be synonymous with Christian service, parents often find no time for walking, talking, working, and playing leisurely with their children. Yet it is just such pursuits as these which contain prime opportunities for spiritual training. The Scriptures teach this. Deuteronomy 6:4-7 and 11:18, 19 instruct parents to teach God's Word throughout the day, from arising until retiring. It should be discussed naturally and spontaneously as part of the normal family conversations—at mealtime, or while sitting in the living room, or while working outside in the yard.

"Look, Mary and Billy. Here's a story in the paper about a boy who died of burns because he ran into a flaming house to rescue his baby sister. When that little girl grows up, she's never going to forget how her brother gave his life for her. What does that remind you of? Let's get the Bible and read John 15:13. Can you think of other Bible passages that talk about this?"

"Hey, Dad, come over here! Quick! There's a nest in the tree by the back fence, and there are tiny birds in it! It reminds me of Psalm 104 that we read in devotions last night. God's creation is really wonderful, isn't it?"

Scenes like these should be a normal part of every Christian home. But they demand time together—unrushed time. Parents must learn to value family life as God does, even if it means saying no to many outside activities. Rearing a child for the Lord Jesus *is* Christian service, and it takes time.

(2) Failure to realize the home's potential. Parents are often unaware of the high premium God places on the home. We see his emphasis on the family in passages such as those mentioned in Deuteronomy. We see it in Proverbs, and in Ephesians 5 and 6 and Colossians 3. Yet when spiritual instruction is mentioned, many parents can think only in terms of the church or outside Christian agencies. They fail to see that God intends for parents to teach their children, who in turn will teach *their* children. This is what God has planned. Notice this pattern in Psalm 78:1-7.

Sometimes we are unaware of the unplanned influence of the

home. Much is caught, even if not explicitly taught—both good and not so good. The child usually spends at least eighteen years in the home. This time element in itself should make parents see the wonderful potential which lies within their walls.

The Indians used to mark trails by bending young saplings so that the trees would grow in a certain direction. We receive our children in the tender, bending stage. In what direction will they grow? We yearn to lead people to salvation and growth in Christ. Yet parents' biggest opportunity lies close at hand. The Master Potter has given us pliable young lives to be molded into "vessels meet for the Master's use."

(3) Lack of confidence. Parents frequently express feelings of inadequacy in matters of Christian education in the home. They realize their children need to learn the Scriptures which are able to make them "wise unto salvation through faith which is in Christ Jesus" (2 Tim. 3:15), but they don't feel that they have the ability to instruct them.

Such parents are like the disciples who sensed the hunger of the five thousand but felt they had no bread to give (Mark 6:35-44). These parents say: "The only hope for our children is to send them to a Christian boarding school, a good Sunday school, a youth camp, meetings and rallies and evangelistic services where they will hear the challenge of missions. At these places they will receive the bread of life. Can anything more be required of us?"

But Jesus told the disciples, "You give them something to eat." This was met by a protest. It would cost too much. Christ assured the disciples that it would cost nothing more than what they had. "How many loaves have ye? Go and see." It seemed so pitifully little, but in the hands of Jesus Christ it was multiplied to more than meet the need.

The prayer of many parents today might be: "Lord, we don't have much either. But we know that we love you, and we want to bring our children to you just as the parents of long ago. Take our meager faith, our personalities, our minds, our imagination—our time. Take what we have and multiply them, and open our eyes to ways we can train up our children in your nurture and admonition."

The Lord commands us to teach his Word diligently to our children (Deut. 6:7). To teach it, we must know it. That means study on the part of parents. Every Christian home should be equipped with tools for Bible study—good commentaries, a Bible dictionary, aids in understanding doctrine, and a concordance. Excellent reading materials abound these days. Christian magazines coming into the home provide spiritual help for family members. But most of all, parents will want to spend much time reading the Bible itself and thinking through its implications for life today. If parents are really enthused about God's Word, that enthusiasm will spill over to their children.

We must stimulate thinking on the part of our youngsters. God told the Israelites how to answer their children's questions. (See Exod. 12:26-27; 13:14-16; and Deut. 6:20-25.) It was taken for granted that the children would ask such questions. If the parents were training as God had said, their children would inevitably think upon these matters. Do we encourage our children to express their questions freely? Do we help them think them through? Or do we quickly try to silence them with a "pat" answer?

We ourselves must mentally ask questions because, as someone has observed, our answers are only as big as the questions we have asked throughout life. Are we prepared for the time when a science-minded little boy will ask, "Daddy, how could Joshua tell the sun to stand still when it's the earth that moves?" Will we be stunned when our teenager asks, "How can we know the Bible is really God's Word? In school we've studied about sacred books other religions have, and they contain great moral teachings, too."

The child who learns to think through these matters under his parents' loving guidance gains experience in dealing with doubts and searching out answers for himself. He is not likely to be tossed about by "every wind of doctrine" when he goes off to college, military service or employment.

Family devotions have too often slipped into a dull pattern in which Father reads from the Bible and a devotional booklet, then leads in prayer. Why not get the whole family involved? Use a Bible story book and ask the children questions—not fact questions ("What are the disciples' names?") but *thought* questions ("Why did Jesus choose the disciples? How does Mark 3:14 apply to us personally?").

Books such as Ken Taylor's *Devotions for the Children's Hour* and *Romans for the Family Hour*, and Concordia's *Little Visits with God* books encourage such thinking together about the Bible's message and life application.

Choose easy-to-understand Bible passages in contemporary translations and have the children read them. Teach a child how to pray by asking, "What was the main point we learned tonight?" Then encourage him to pray with that in mind.

If Christ is the real Head of your home, your children will walk safely in the world. ●

Handwashed Dishes Are Best by Joy Scheifele

Mommy, I know what I'm going to get you for your birthday," our seven-year-old announced recently.

"Oh?"

"A dishwasher!" he triumphantly promised.

His motives, however, were not purely altruistic. It was his turn that night to help with the supper dishes. No doubt the stack of dirty dishes did resemble the proverbial mountain to his young eyes, tired after a day of hard play. To him a dishwasher seemed the perfect solution.

When our three children had all entered school, it seemed the appropriate time to my husband and me to help them learn responsibility—and to appreciate the efforts of others. Consequently, to help us reach our goal we tried experimenting with the plan of having each of the three take turns helping with the supper dishes. It is their choice to either wash or dry. But one child and I work side by side on the chore.

"I hate dishes" is not an uncommon complaint.

"Nor is it my favorite pastime," I quickly remind them.

Once they have gotten that feeling off their chests (or is it becoming a sort of ritual?) things generally settle down quickly, and I have discovered this to be one of the best times for quiet discussion and sharing.

All three—Leigh, now eleven; Monica, nine; and Andrew, seven—eagerly relate what has taken place at school over the evening meal with both mom and dad present. However, with a tea towel in their hand later, they will frequently confide fears, expectations, and disappointments while the two of us work together in the quiet kitchen.

With only one helping each evening, I have found that it is a foolproof method of insuring a half hour of time with each at least twice a week. While bedtime is another good time for conversation, frequent evening meetings and other commitments make it less reliable. Also, as our children grow older, the bedtime-story routine which usually naturally leads into time for quiet discussion has been replaced with time spent reading by themselves as they've discovered the pleasures of books on their own.

Through their sharing I have become keenly aware of how they are struggling to grow up, of how difficult that struggle can be for them. By providing an opportunity for them to talk over some of their problems in a related setting, we can offer reassurance and guidance in a way that is quite natural.

One of their common complaints when I'm washing and they are drying is: "Mommy, don't go so fast." It is rarely a job to get through as quickly as possible for them. Rather it seems often to have a soothing effect—especially if they are washing. The warm sudsy water can be pleasant if we but only let it. As adults we frequently tend to disregard the pleasant aspects in face of the dirt and mess that needs to be cleaned away.

Nor is the task assigned only to the children and myself. Sunday mornings Nelson takes his turn, as well as at other times when it is necessary for me to leave immediately following the meal.

Whenever we invite friends for a meal, we do not object in the least to our guests helping! Such occasions are truly times of fellowship. Many of our friendships have deepened over the kitchen sink.

The children also witness the great amount of "visiting" which is done in the kitchen of the church following a potluck meal. Often both mothers and fathers pitch in with dishcloths and tea towels returning things to order.

Each of our children reacts differently to various situations and responds differently to those around. This is what makes bringing them up such a fascinating, challenging, but often difficult task.

We've discovered each needs to have time alone with both my husband and me to grow. Such moments are often needed to help interpret the child to himself, to help him understand himself better, and to recognize his own personal strengths.

Subjects tend to take a wide range over the dishpan. I recall when Leigh inquired many years ago, "Why did Jesus have to die on the cross? Why couldn't he have stayed alive so we could see him to-day?"

"What do the ants do in the winter?" our youngest wondered as the snow was falling outside. He has always had a keen interest in the garden.

Nor is it always conversation. Sometime it is an appropriate time to practice new songs learned either at school or church. I find this to be most pleasant and relaxing.

We find each of the three extremely sensitive individuals. We feel a responsibility to help insure that their sensitivity is channeled in a positive way. A few weeks ago Monica was ill, running a very high fever over the supper hour. Andrew was scheduled to help with the dishes that evening. While I was caring for his sister, he quietly both washed and dried the dishes, freeing me of the responsibility so I could be with Monica when she most needed me.

And so, my dear little Andrew, thank you, but please don't worry about buying me a dishwasher for my birthday! No convenience in the world is worth the time I now spend with you, Monica, and Leigh as we work together on those dirty dishes!　●

The Education of My Babies' Mother by Marilyn McGinnis

The birth of our daughter occurred two weeks after the publication of my first book. To commemorate the book's debut, the publisher sent me an enormous bouquet of red roses. For days their beauty filled the dining area of our tiny duplex. My husband and I smelled their sweet fragrance, admired the rich red color, and rejoiced at the impending birth of our child.

Quite frankly, I haven't seen a rose since.

The day our daughter arrived, life changed for George and Marilyn McGinnis as it had never changed before. The carefree lifestyle of a couple who could invite friends over (or be invited) on a whim, go out for pizza at midnight, read or type manuscripts for two hours uninterrupted came to a screeching halt.

The anticipation of parenthood gave way rather quickly to the realities of parenthood.

When she was hungry, she was hungry. It never occurred to her that we might be hungry, tired, busy, or anything else. She wanted to be fed right now!

When she was wet (or worse), she was wet. And she wanted to be changed. Now! Not whenever Mom or Dad got around to it.

If she decided that three A.M. was playtime, then it was playtime. Neither bottles, nor pacifiers, nor logical reasoning could convince her otherwise. She was in charge.

Twenty-two months later our once carefree lifestyle was pushed even further into never-never land. On a July summer evening our two baby boys arrived, one right after the other. We thought we were busy with one!

Gone (for awhile) is adult entertaining. Gone are most of the spur-of-the-moment pleasures. Gone is uninterrupted *anything*. To be a mother is never to finish a sentence—or the dishes. In the few brief moments I have been sitting here typing, both boys (now age three) have brought me a hilarious report of how "Daddy carried us both in one towel (from the bathtub) to the bedroom!" and one boy showing me his pajama dilemma (also considered highly amusing)—bottoms on, tops rolled hopelessly around his chest, neck stretched completely out of shape.

An *hour* of solitude has been compromised for a *moment* of solitude—eagerly sought, quickly recognized, and cherished as if it were to last a lifetime.

Some days, in a mixture of humor and despair, I ask of whomever happens to be listening, "Now why was it I wanted to have children?"

Because, despite all the hard work and frustration, children add a fullness and richness to life that can never be found anywhere else. Holding your own child in your arms and realizing that this tiny helpless infant is bone of your bone and flesh of your (and your mate's) flesh produces a bond of togetherness that only the Creator could bestow. It is that fulfillment of a lifetime. It simply was meant to be.

Because I like being a family. The hardest thing about being single was not belonging to anybody. My parents lived several hundred miles away and there were no relatives nearby to whom I was close. The loneliness of those years was often filled in part by—a family. A wonderful family of five who took me in whenever I needed to be taken, and made me feel like one of them. I like being part of a family.

That, too, was meant to be.

Because I told God when I was very young that I didn't want an easy life. I want to grow in my Christian experience and come ever closer to him. What better tool can God use to accomplish that goal than through the trials and tribulations of parenting? The onslaught of motherhood has taught me a lot about myself—some good, some bad.

Getting along as a family is where the rubber meets the road.

The transition from "married" to parenthood is a joyous one. But it is not easy. As I talk with other parents of preschoolers, I find a goodly number of adjustments in thinking and in doing that parents must make when the children begin to arrive.

Some of the adjustments are happy ones.

25

"Becoming a mother was much better, more joyful and fulfilling than I expected."

"It's nice to have another person to love you, especially when the baby first begins responding to you. I love watching babies grow up."

"When they first begin to respond to you, you really appreciate being a parent."

"Having children taught us more about God's love for us. He must have some of the same feelings about us that we have for our children."

"Becoming a mother was the accomplishment of a life goal."

"The unexpected things kids do and say are so special."

"I love watching the beginning of their spiritual relationships, their unshakable faith in God."

Children are rewarding, fulfilling, the challenge of a lifetime.

Some of the adjustments of parenthood, however, are difficult. Before the first child is born there are apprehensions. I wonder how I'll do as a parent. Will I know what to do with such a tiny creature? What will I do the first time he gets sick?

Will I love the baby? How do I know I've got a maternal/paternal instinct when I've never experienced it?

There are apprehensions about our mates. "I really wondered how my husband would do as a father," says my friend Eleanor. "He was very happy with just the two of us. He thought it was fun without children."

Once their daughter arrived, however, her apprehensions faded. Her husband adored their daughter. "Now," she says happily, "he wonders what on earth life would be like without Brenda."

And, of course, there are apprehensions about the child to be born.

Will he/she be healthy?

What if he has Down's syndrome, or is deformed, or sickly?

Would we know how to cope?

Once the child arrives, the apprehensions begin to fade. In their place come a whole new set of adjustments.

None of us is fully prepared for the amount of *time* it takes to be a parent. In theory I knew that babies took a lot of time. But until our daughter arrived I had never experienced it. And it took a while for it to sink in. I naively thought that life could go on pretty much as usual.

Within a few days after baby's arrival you begin to realize your loss of freedom, that feeling of being tied down. No longer can you pick up and go at the slightest whim to shop, visit a friend, or have a romantic dinner out with your husband. Suddenly you are a slave to the demands of a very tiny human being who controls your every action.

How well I recall the morning it took three hours to get my two babies and one toddler ready for an outing. By the time I got each one fed, changed and dressed, somebody had spit up, wet, messed his/her pants, or needed another bottle and it was time to start all over again!

You must also adjust to the limited amount of time you can spend together as husband and wife. Your husband had a meeting at work that he really wants to discuss with you. But that's when the baby starts screaming with colic.

You reach lovingly for each other in the middle of the night, only to discover the warm body of your toddler lodged comfortably between you. You don't even know what hour of the night he climbed in.

You're dying to discuss some current event but the children are bubbling with news about *their* day's events. Before children, you rarely had to plan time together. Now it becomes a necessity.

You must also adjust your expectations of how you, your mate, and your children will react in the real-life situations of family life. Before I had children I was such a quiet soul, even quite shy in my younger years. Since becoming a parent I have been transformed, at times, into a raving maniac. I never saw that side of myself before—and neither did my husband! He is a rather mild-mannered man himself, but there are days when the children push his back to the wall as well.

I will never scream at my children, I said (before I had any). That was before I discovered that children are born deaf, hard of hearing or, at best, practice selective hearing. When the vibrations from a good scream have captured their attention, then you can speak to them in a normal tone of voice. But it's "not my nature" to scream.

Another adjustment comes when we try to correlate what we've been "taught" about raising children with life as it really is.

One of the first things I did when I became a parent was to throw out just about everything I had ever learned concerning child rearing. A few sound principles do remain lodged in my cranium because I have proven them to be true. But a lot of theory written by people who probably never had children just doesn't cut it. Neither does some of the advice offered by well-meaning relatives and friends.

Parenthood is a course each of us plows for himself.

With three children under the age of two, *I faced a serious adjustment in accepting my own limitations.* I used to be so self-sufficient. There wasn't much I couldn't handle myself. Suddenly I'm dissolving in tears at the slightest provocation from overwork, lack of sleep, and an around-the-clock feeding schedule. Even with a lot of help from my husband, he still had to go to work (or we wouldn't eat) and he most assuredly had to get a reasonable amount of sleep at night (or he wouldn't be *able* to go to work). The solution, of course, was to hire help.

Hire help? Me? But I've always done my own housework. I've always taken care of the children myself. Another adjustment which, like any, has its own rewards. "Help" turned out to be a wonderful lady who has enriched our lives a thousand times over, and out-of-state grandparents who lighten the load considerably with their several-times-a-year visits.

During the first year with our boys I learned to *accept* help, as well as to give it.

That, for me, was a valuable lesson.

Each child added to the family brings added joy—and added tension—in any family situation. Occasionally we are able to spend time alone with just one of our children. Almost without exception, as soon as we have that child alone to ourselves, life suddenly becomes serene. Gone is the bickering over who wore the Superman pajamas last night and whose turn it is to pick up the toys in the living room. The "only" child has no one to fight with and has no need to compete for mom and dad's attention. He/she is a different child—and we are different parents.

I don't for a moment regret having three children. But I also recognize that the more little ones you add to your home, the more opportunity there is for tension.

The psalmist advised, "How good and how pleasant it is for brothers to live harmoniously together!" (Ps. 133:1, *Berkeley*). What he doesn't say is how long it takes to produce that happy cohabitation! ●

Songs for Caged-in Mothers by Gayle Roper

"I love my children, Lord, but if I can't get out of the house once in a while, I'll go crazy!"

Every mother faces a time when she literally is housebound by her children. They become little golden links that chain her relentlessly to her home. She resents the bondage, feels frustrated by it and guilty about. Sometimes coping is almost more than she can handle.

Today's Christian woman is better educated and more articulate and opinionated than ever before. From childhood she's been taught to think for herself and form opinions. More often than not she's been financially independent because of a job. Innumerable church activities, secular activities from spectator sports to shopping, and the constant flow of entertaining have geared her to a rather frantic pace of living. Often the first pre-child years of marriage give her her greatest mobility. Then, boom. It's home with baby.

No matter how much the baby was wanted, feelings of confinement arise. The little ones bring with their adoring coos and goos a restriction the young mother has not known before.

How these feelings of restriction are handled makes all the difference in the quality of mothering. A woman either becomes a mother who passes on to her family the joy of the Lord through her example or a mother who crabs and complains.

A woman must realize that her caged-in feelings are no cause for guilt. They are merely the result of her change in life styles. These feelings are as predictable as bends to a diver who surfaces too quickly. Moving out of one environment into another too speedily produces a shock to one's system.

For a Christian mother, the major responsibility in life is the training of her children. It is not a duty she should surrender without careful consideration. The option of escaping her home by working is only to be considered as a last resort. In some situations the mother with young children has no recourse.

So there you are, a young Christian mother with a house full of children, a head full of knowledge about your duty to them, and a heart full of rebellion. What do you do?

Begin by talking to the Lord about it, no holds barred. Tell him your guilt feelings. It's certainly healthier for you to give him your sour feelings than to throw them in your husband's face or to serve them to your children with dinner.

Don't think that laying a problem of this magnitude before the Lord once in a fit of anger or anguish is enough. Do it again and again in a quiet manner. Share with him the scope of your feelings. Perhaps the only place for solitude is the bathroom or shower. So be it.

"Lord, I need help. Please give me creative outlets and ideas with which to solve my problem because I know it won't go away. And I don't really want it to go away because that would mean no kids. So how do I work around my predicament?"

Remember 1 Corinthians 10:13? God promised not to let us be tempted above our ability to take it. He further promised ways of escape which will enable us to survive. These promises apply to a housebound mother as much as to anyone.

Remember the abundant life promised to believers in John 10:10? This life is offered to the weary, child-chained mother, just as it is to other believers. If you're too tired or tense to experience this abundance then something is wrong. With the Lord's help, you must correct it.

After you and the Lord are thoroughly conversant about your feelings, mixed as they are, talk to your husband. Often a man doesn't realize how squelched you feel. He hasn't had the experience of blowing runny noses all winter or refereeing endless arguments or trying to converse with a three-year-old.

Gently remind him that he meets people all day, that he has conversations on an adult level, and even has time to think. Ask him to at least consider with you possible escape hatches. After all, he wants you functioning at peak competency. He has a vested interest in helping you.

Now begin to think practically about your personal situation. Ask the Lord to give you workable ideas. Keep in mind your limitations. You still have a home to maintain. You still have your children to raise. You're not looking for total escape, just occasional outlets. There are all kinds of possibilities.

Industrious women can often find ways to earn money at home. Meg designs and sells delightful crewel kits to local department stores and teaches craft courses in her home.

Marjorie found she could put her secretarial training to work and be a public stenographer to small businesses and clubs unable to afford their own secretaries. She sets her own hours and work load. All she needs is a small corner of her home for her equipment.

Other services offer no money, but honor the Lord. Edith babysat for the Bible study. Pam used to give me one afternoon a week. She would bring her kids to my house and watch mine, thereby freeing me to spend the time in the library to write in peace and quiet.

A Christian can find many church ministries and services. Alternating weeks with your husband in attending prayer meetings gives you both a chance to take part in the service. Perhaps with very young children, you will also have to alternate Sunday nights.

The best way to prevent stagnation is to offer your own service. And what better place can you find than your church? Marilyn finds her outlet in the church library. She brings her young children and lets them play in the church nursery while she catalogs and files. Gay also serves as her church librarian, but she does all her work at home.

Extension or night courses may offer a positive remedy for boredom for you. Sue took a course in decoupage. Edith and Arlene studied sewing. Joanne studied watercolors and egg tempera painting. She's now beginning a course in quilting. Pam took a mail-order course in home decorating. I studied writing by extension. Marie and Agnes took Bible correspondence courses.

One caution. When time weighs heavily on your hands or boredom makes you lethargic, don't let yourself become addicted to daytime TV. Not only are these programs a waste of time, but the type of life they depict is the antithesis of that which a Christian should be living.

In all the planning to find time for yourself, don't overlook finding time to spend with the Lord. Perhaps it will have to be like Mildred who had not only children to cope with but also a husband who was antagonistic toward the gospel. The only place she could be certain of being uninterrupted was the bathroom. That's where she prayed and read her Bible.

Pat developed a program of reading a few Bible verses a day and writing down five specific prayer requests. About five minutes was all she could be certain of, but it kept her consistent and close to the Lord.

Consider carefully the following questions. Which is more important to the smooth and happy functioning of a home: a spotless house or a contented homemaker? Which is the better welcome to a tired husband at day's end: an immaculate house or a cheery wife with something positive to share? Which is more important in teaching the little ones: a carping mother who lectures in discontent and boredom or a smiling mother who shares from her personal feeling of accomplishment?

We've all been created in the image of a Creator. Therefore we are creative beings. If we neglect this aspect of our personalities, we feel stifled, flat, bored. The trick for the housebound mother is to find ways to be creative and free within the limitations of her life. It can be done. It must be done if she ever hopes to hear those beautiful words, "Her children arise up, and call her blessed; her husband also, and he praiseth her" (Prov. 31:28). ●

Parents Play to Win by Robert C. Rayburn

Christian families should pray together, but they should also play together! Children cannot develop properly and possess well-balanced personalities without adequate time for recreation. The old adage is still true that "all work and no play makes Jack a dull boy."

If it is important for the children to have time to play, it is also vital that they should have the pleasure of one and preferably both of their parents participating in their fun. The parent who plays with his children will discover not only genuine benefits for the children but also a renewing experience for himself.

While educational games do not provide the release of energy often needed by young children, they are most desirable. One of my sons learned the names of four literary works for each of eight or ten masters of English prose before he could even read! Eager to play "Authors" with his older brother and sisters, he quickly memorized the books for each author.

Such games as "Scrabble" and the newer "Spill and Spell" not only teach spelling, enlarge vocabulary, and sharpen wits, but are great fun. Games of this type are much more profitable than those which move an object around a board according to the throw of dice or the spin of a pointer.

The intelligent adult who plays "brain" games with his children will teach them without using his superior knowledge to win continually and removing the "game" from the contest.

Any child who shows a willingness to learn intricacies should be encouraged to play chess. This wonderful game develops one's capacity for reasoning as well as powers of observation and keenness of foresight. It should not be played casually, but children can develop real skill in it.

No Christian family should be without a good selection of Bible

games. It is amazing how many facts concerning the Scriptures can be stored up in young minds through the pleasant activity afforded by the best Bible games. Care should be taken in the selection of them as poor Bible games can dull the interest of children in the Word of God.

In addition to indoor games, every family needs some participation in sports which develop the body perhaps more than the mind. The well-rounded child needs good physical coordination and a strong, healthy body.

Some sports are highly competitive. Others, like swimming, are not or at least need not be. Swimming is not only a delightful and beneficial form of exercise; it is a skill which may be needed for the preservation of life. Many communities can afford a swimming pool even if natural beaches are not available. What could be better than for the parents to learn to swim, if necessary, at the same time as the children? A display of good sportsmanship would endear the older to the younger.

If there is room in the yard, every sizeable family should try a volleyball court. Although this game provides vigorous exercise, it is not too strenuous for most adults and can be greatly enjoyed by a mixture of children and older people.

One of the best times for parents to play with their children is the evening period before the youngest children are put to bed. If the family has gathered for worship and the children have participated with the adults, a brief time of play will kindle family unity in a unique way.

Good recreation is not all play! Reading good books is an excellent example of individual recreation. Parents should diligently attend to the reading habits of their children. Encouragement and guidance are important.

Reading a truly good book aloud will be both pleasant and profitable. This excellent practice of previous generations should be revived.

Good music will also contribute to the enjoyment of family recreation hours. Thoughtful parents will cultivate their children's appreciation of great music. A good record collection will help. Attendance at concerts where noted artists perform is an excellent family activity.

If limited finances prevent the building of a record library or attendance at concerts, home-made music is within the reach of all. A family choir can be great fun! The child who develops an appreciation for good music and the ability to play or sing even moderately well is never without something to do.

One other important family activity needs to be mentioned: every family should travel together! It is not always possible to take long vacation trips, but there are many delightful places within a day's travel.

Careful planning will make it possible for a family of even limited means to travel. Camping delights the children and is a wholesome change for adults. Picnic meals can be prepared more easily and as inexpensively at a mountain or seashore retreat as the regular meals at home.

There are places of scenic grandeur and historic interest in all sections of the country. Visits to them will broaden the outlook of children and incite a deeper appreciation of education.

Time that the family spends together in the car can be constructive and enjoyable if well planned. As all share the interests of the journey and each other they are welded together in understanding and love.

Christian parents, take the time and make the effort to improve your family's recreation and thus add spice to all your associations together. ●

Parents Are For Children by Marilou Pittman Weaver

While still single, I knew just how children should be raised.

"Why, if that child were mine he wouldn't act like that," I told myself when I saw a three-year-old hit his mother or scream his defiance at her request.

I didn't realize then how little I understood about child rearing. It took two children of my own to set me straight. Lori is now four and Scotty is two—but already they show minds of their own. Wilful, often stubborn, they force me to ask myself: *How can I raise my children so that they grow up well-adjusted, loving one another and serving God?*

While pondering this one day, my thoughts spun back to my own childhood. What had made our family such a close-knit one? How had we developed such a love for the Lord, such a desire to serve him?

As I sorted out my memories, I recalled some principles my parents had followed in training my brother, sister and me.

As MK's (missionaries' kids), some might say that our environment was less than ideal. We traveled a lot, spending winters in Mexico and summers in Canada.

Because of their work, both Mother and Dad were away from home a good part of each day. When I was ten, I stayed in the States with my grandparents and continued my schooling. I saw my family about every two years, since by now they were working in Australia and the Philippines. And yet, the bond between the five of us always has been close.

In the flood of memories, several principles (all adaptable) stood out.

First, Mom and Dad spent time with us each day.

Dad, especially, was busy with his work, yet he always saved the

38

half hour right after supper for us children. We would climb on his lap and listen to stories or poetry and memorize Bible verses.

My last year in college, Mother stayed in the States with us while Dad was in Vietnam. Late-evening snacks became family socials. Over hot buttered toast and cocoa, we discussed everything from why we lost the basketball game to, "Is it harder to be a Christian in a Christian school?" These were delightful—often hilarious—times.

Dad often took us downtown to watch the colorful parades that wound through the streets of Mexico City. We thrilled to the holiday fun of happy thoughts, brilliantly colored floats, bands, acrobats and jugglers, and the treat of cotton candy or sugared peanuts.

Back in the States, Dad took us to aquariums and museums, enjoying them as much as we did.

In all of these things he showed without words how much he cared for us.

Dad took advantage of unexpected opportunities to enjoy and teach his children.

We never traveled leisurely. We invariably had a three-day trip to make in two, and we had many such trips during the year.

Dad and Mother joined in our games—Bible and history quizzes, "I'm thinking of something," or "I see more animals on my side than you do on yours." Tiring of this, we would all join in singing.

When I was seven, it was my job to do the supper dishes. But Dad helped. I washed and he dried. Dad made games of the arithmetic tables and I learned them before I even realized what was happening.

For a while, we lived in a small village south of Mexico City. Our house was not elegant—a two-room adobe brick with a dirt floor—but it was home. One day Dad finally trapped a wily rat that had for days evaded capture. Taking us all out to a table in the back yard, he gave us our first anatomy lesson, carefully dissecting the animal as he explained each part in detail.

Instead of pitying us for all we missed by not living in the States, my parents encouraged us to explore and make use of the world around us.

We had few toys—nothing like the fantastic variety children have today. Yet I had a delightful childhood. My parents encouraged me to improvise from my environment. Castor beans from the plants near the house and milkweed silk made excellent food for my dolls

39

or medicine for their ills. Thorn-bush spikes substituted for hypo needles, and with some maneuvering I managed to fit two pieces of slender corn stalk together for the barrel and plunger.

As I grew older, Dad showed me how to weave beaded bracelets on a handmade loom and mother taught me to cook, crochet, knit and tat. I was extremely proud the day when—with Mother's help—I baked a white cake, frosted it, and took it over to our friends. Of course it did sag a little in the middle.

"Just the way I like it," Dad commented.

"Fill it with frosting," was Mother's solution.

Dad and Mom always listened to our problems. They won our confidence when we were small so we continued to share our joys and trials with them as we grew older.

When we lived in Mexico City, Dad's office and our home were in the same building so we could go to him at any time. Sometimes he would offer a solution, but often he encouraged us to think of one for ourselves.

As a teen, I wrote mother about the frustrations I encountered in a new school. Even though half a world away, she always answered and gave advice.

Mother used current happenings to give advice long before we needed it.

Once I heard Mother talking to a friend. A mutual girl friend's husband had left her without support for their eight children. Everyone had advised against the mixed marriage, but she had disregarded their counsel. Turning to me, Mother said, "Honey, I want you to remember this and be very careful to marry just the man the Lord has for you."

"But, Mother," I protested, "I won't get married for years and years! I'm only ten, you know."

"Yes, I know," she answered, "but I'm telling you now when you'll listen. When you're older, it may be too late." I never forgot the incident.

Both Mother and Dad prayed daily for us . . . and we knew it. This was most important of all.

Family devotions each evening were an integral part of our lives which, as we grew older, encouraged us in our private devotions. Even now that I am married and have a family of my own, I know Mother and Dad pray specifically for each of us—I can see the evidence in our lives.

Their example of God's love in their lives made a big impression on me. They taught and showed me that only in God's will can anyone be truly happy.

Perhaps these are some of the reasons I have followed in their footsteps and my husband and I also are missionaries.

As I watch my small children play—and sometimes fight—together, I often wonder what kind of people they'll grow up to be. I think back to my own childhood. The principles applied then will guide me in rearing Lori and Scotty. It will take time—but the development of a godly man and woman will be worth it.

More than ever I realize that with God's help, if we train up our children in the way they should go, when they are old they will not depart from it. ●

Strategy for the Family by Ted Ward

A title in *The New Republic* recently caught my eye: "The Obsolete Home." Perhaps, I thought, here is a major piece in the popular press acknowledging that the family is outdated, a relic of past history.

No, the article was concerned instead with changes in housing patterns due largely to inflation. But not to inflation alone, as I saw. It asserted: ". . . the post-war children aren't behaving like their parents: they're marrying later, divorcing more often, having fewer children, and sending both men and women to work—factors that may weaken the lure of the single-family home." Things are changing indeed.

Several months ago I told a group of psychologists and educators that the school is not the best institution for promoting moral values in our society. The family is crucial, and to assume that the church is dead is to be misled by appearances. As I finished, I expected the discussion to center on my contention that the church is still alive as an instrument of human welfare. To my surprise, the discussion immediately attacked my "archaic" and "quaint" view that the *family* can be expected to play a significant role in values development.

It was like watching a turning point of history. Here were American and Canadian scholars arguing that the family as we have known it is disappearing.

If secular society is ready to abandon the family as a defunct institution, Christians are not. I suggest at least three conclusions:

1. In the Christian community, the family remains basic.

2. The Christian family is well on the way to being distinctly different from the secular family (or whatever substitute for the family the secular society may create).

3. Pressures upon the "odd" Christian family can have strengthening outcomes for the church.

The first reality is essentially theological, and can be supported scripturally. The second is sociological, and can be observed by anyone alert to what the "body-life" ministries, for example, are helping Christian families to become. The third point is admittedly speculative, though it can be supported on historical grounds. The history of Christianity reminds us that Christ is glorified and the church grows through adversity.

Scientists have two quite different ways to respond to social trends. The most common is to shrug and say, "That's the way it is." But the scientist who draws his moral premises from spiritual sources does not accept what exists as necessarily the way things ought to be.

As a Christian, I see trends that I don't like, can't accept, and must work against. I cannot expect secular society to share my concerns, yet I must do more than make the best of things. I must take a particular responsibility for my own family and also share responsibilities for the families of the church of our Lord. We are salt in the general society, but we are *members* of one another in the body of Christ. As Christians, we have decisions to make, things to reject, things to embrace, and on some issues we need to *fight*. (If we accept the instruction of the Word, we won't often be fighting *against each other!*)

The key institutions of society are ordained by God, according to the Scriptures: the church (Matt. 16:18), the family (Eph. 5 and 6), and the civil government (Rom. 13). But that doesn't mean that every family is godly, every government is righteous, or every religious organization is approved by God. The Christian family is part of the larger social institution of family—the Christian distinctive is in honoring Christ by establishing a particular kind of family. If we get that straight, we won't need to worry greatly about secular influences.

I am more concerned about erosion than frontal attacks. We Christians can handle the head-on attacks of evil in the society, but the subtle undercutting and washing away in bits and pieces is most dangerous. In a materialistic society where one's worth is measured by his properties, the Christian can be gradually pushed into forgetting Jesus' teaching: "Lay not up for yourselves treasures upon earth . . ." (Matt. 6:20). A question mark must be placed over the

44

ways we stimulate our children to succeed—even the ways we lay up treasure in order to provide them a "good education" and a "good start in life."

As if television's constant bombardment with lewd sex were not enough, a greater threat comes in the form of situation comedies and variety shows that emphasize infidelity and intellectual competitiveness in marriage. Laughing at human frailties may have some therapeutic value, but the larger effect is to condition a person to accept as normal the bickering, competitive, and spiteful behavior that fractures marriages.

We must stand with those who seek justice, including fair play and equal opportunity. Thus I join in seeking liberation from secular customs that give men special authority and power over women in an unbiblical way.

But I caution my fellow-liberators that for women to share the competitive, dog-eat-dog system of the "man's world" will be a hollow victory. Far better to work as Christians to reduce the ailment in the male role that results in his need to dominate.

Closely related is the pressure of the public schools to conform and compete. Schooling in the pervasive Greek model is inherently success-oriented. But the Christian is to see individuality not in terms of "betterness" but in terms of gifts that the Spirit gives for the benefit of others. This calls for development as a cooperative, serving sort of person ("For the love of Christ controls us" . . . 2 Cor. 5:14).

The school is not a unique influence or threat. The "business world" and sometimes even the church tend to decide what is right by asking what works.

Pragmatism and relativism have particularly assaulted marriage. Vows once said for life are being replaced by fingers-crossed generalizations that are to be respected as long as they work out, or until something "better" comes along.

The Christian family can guard itself by helping children see marriage in the best possible light, by spending time together reading God's Word and discussing its meaning, and by arriving at moral judgments together.

We live in one of the most materialistic societies in history. Unhappiness, even to the extremes of suicide and divorce, results from placing hope, confidence, and pride in the products of a mechanistic society.

Some North Americans are becoming aware of the horrible ecological effects of over-consumption and waste. Society's economic foundation rests on consumerism, and its children are taught to buy-buy-buy, eat-eat-eat, and go-go-go, or the whole thing will fall apart.

Materialism causes us to value *things* more than *people*. Our competitive greed and self-centered individualism cut deeply into our realization of true community within the body of Christ!

Antidotes to materialism within the Christian family include encouraging cooperative experiences; setting non-materialistic goals as a family; deciding together what is enjoyable and profitable; and affirming one another as being worthy.

Faulty communication styles of secular institutions are tending to dehumanize us. We see the effects in "communication gaps" or "generation gaps." Research in values development reveals that there is a close relationship between communication styles in the child's experiences and the development of higher structures of values.

God began his relationship with us who share his image by walking and talking in the garden. Today we understand that a child's moral development depends on a freedom to communicate, to share, to seek counsel, and to know the accepting fellowship of a parent who is ready to talk through the dilemmas and the times of confusion.

The Christian family can bridge communication problems by listening to one another with non-judgmental openness, and by developing warm communication styles while the going is good. Then communication will be open when rough moments occur.

As the Word of God is pushed further and further from the center of human reasoning, injustice becomes more common. The prophets were sent time and again with God's call to repentance. Scholars point out that *righteousness* cannot be defined apart from *justice*. Let us lift our voices against injustice wherever it is seen.

We live in a society where authority seems equivalent to righteousness, and our families are threatened.

Somehow we must see that God's justice, love, and mercy become central characteristics of our life style and family relationships. If secular society abandons the family, the renewed Christian home will shine all the brighter! ●

We Grew With Our Children by Betty Garton Ulrich

Did you ever clean out a storage space and find something which seemed almost beyond price because of the memories it evoked? This happened to me when I came upon a folder of "minutes" written ten years ago by the older two of our five children. As I leafed through the folder, memories flooded over me. I had suggested a weekly family meeting because I believed that if the children had a chance to air their grievances and had a hand in the planning of their chores, privileges and punishments, they would be more cooperative and feel greater responsibility. Since Barbie at 9 and Jim at 8 were the only two old enough to write, they took turns being "secretary." Ruthie, 6, and John, 4, were allowed to take turns "chairing" the meetings. David, 2, was happy just to sit up and watch. The big event for him was getting his weekly allowance. One of the first meetings, recorded meticulously, was typical:

October 17, 1958. James called the meeting to order. The secretary read the minutes and the forfited money was put into the treasury. There was know old buisness. New busness: it was decided that if Jimmy and Barbara fought in the kitchen they would each have to clear (the table) once by themselves. It was also decided that if we got into any big fights 2¢ is to be docked and Mother can punish us in any way she sees fit. We are all going to be good so we can go to the muzeum and zoo. It was moved and seconded that the meeting be adgurned. The amount in our treasury is 38¢. Respectfully submitted, Barbara.

As I read, it seemed almost impossible that the little girl who wrote it is now a 20-year-old who worked and saved her money for two and a half years so she could enroll in a special school of horsemanship. Or that Jim, her doughty kitchen opponent of yesteryear, is now a 19-year-old in his second year on a large scholarship at Yale University.

48

At one meeting, the secretary had recorded: *The new busness was Johnny's destructiveness.*

As I reminisced, I remembered that Johnny had been going through a difficult period which was really my fault. I had been working half-days and had a "competent" babysitter to care for John and David, the only two not in school. One day my husband returned home unexpectedly to find David, a husky child of 2, pounding 4-year-old John on the head with a toy truck.

The babysitter, placidly ironing, said, "Oh, they do that all the time. It don't bother me none."

John, of course, had been taught that little boys are not supposed to act that way, while David was just at the age where he should have been learning it at the hands of a concerned mother.

John, with too much conscience to beat his baby brother back, but too immature to cope with him on any other level, soon began to take out his resentment and frustration in sneaky and destructive ways. One day we saw him in the garden beating the heads off a row of flowers with a thick stick. I quit work soon after that. My job, I felt, was to spend my time in the daily training of my children. There was no one else whose job it really ought to be. I was never sorry for that decision. By circumventing David's aggressive attacks and praising John for his patience with his "little brother," I found that John's feeling of angry frustration against David slowly melted.

It was only a year later, his aggressiveness not diminished, but channeled into more constructive areas, that David said lovingly to his older but basically shyer brother, "Tum on, Donny, don't be afwaid. I'll take 'oo to Sunny 'cool." And so, although for weeks before that, John had refused to go to the Sunday School in the new town to which we'd moved, he allowed David, just turned 3, to lead him down the aisle, right to the front row.

Paging through the minutes, I found that I often was not consistent in my discipline. Barbara recorded on February 6, 1959: *Mother also said that this was the last time she was going to egnore the allowance deducsions.*

There were, I discovered, plenty of occasions for allowance deductions. Jim wrote once, with his inimitable spelling: *The olowanants was handed out and the deducscions were put in the tressary. Total in our tressary is now 88¢.*

A sheet of paper with notations in my writing revealed the following aberrations and penalties:

Oct. 12—Jim: Sunday clothes wadded up on bathroom floor—2¢
Oct. 16—Barbie: threw jacket on closet floor—2¢
Oct. 17—Barbie: bad behavior in kitchen—2¢
Oct. 30—Ruthie fighting with Barbie—2¢
Nov. 4—Ruth and Jim: fighting over TV—each 2¢

On another occasion, the minutes revealed that *we discused differnt ways to make supper time more intersting. It was decided that a couple times every week we discus som topic and let Father and Mother tell us something more about it.*

I couldn't remember any of the specific topics we discussed, but I was surprised to realize that our many discussions in recent years at our dinner table (on religion, morality, current events, etc.) undoubtedly had their beginnings way back there when our oldest child was only 9.

Since the day I discovered the little notebook, I've done a lot of thinking. I know we've made many mistakes in rearing our children. I've probably been too strict many times. I know I've "jawed" at them much more than was necessary. And yet, I don't think we've made any drastic mistakes. They all are conscientious, responsible, honest children, growing up with a strong family feeling for each other. While they have their spats, they do not carry on the bitter, downgrading rivalry among themselves that I notice in some families.

They are respectful to their elders, do well in school, and do not, any of them, drink or smoke. They seem to have accepted our ultimatum that until they are full-grown and of legal age, we call the plays. But such "arbitrary" control on our part does not seem to have stunted either their characters or their personalities: they are healthy, happy, normally rebellious kids.

I often thank God that we were given these five children. And I am glad we also were given the courage and faith to stick to the things we knew were right and good, even when other parents were letting down the bars: letting their children have too much freedom with too little guidance; ignoring rudeness, bad behavior, slovenliness, and downright immorality.

If our experience has taught us anything, it is that children

51

need—and respond to—love, attention, discipline, and consistent living and teaching.

I'm glad, too, that my husband kept insisting, "You can't always say 'No!' to kids without giving them something positive to do." And then he'd buy (sometimes when we could ill afford it) fishing tackle or photography equipment or canvases and paints and teach our children how to use them.

The years have gone so fast. And some of them were hard: when the children were little all at once, when we didn't have enough money to go around, when someone always was sick. Yet I wouldn't change any of it, because while we were struggling and praying we were really forming character (both ours and the children's) and were building memories, too.

But above all, I realize now how deeply we have relied on our Christian faith. We have based our lives and our teaching of the children on this faith. We always have had family devotions and regular churchgoing. My husband even wrote a book of family devotions because he could not find anything that was meaningful to all the ages in our family. Augsburg published it, and our children have grown up with the book.

We taught our children that only if man is a spiritual as well as a physical being is there any sense to morality. But if he is a spiritual being, then nothing makes any sense without the Judeo-Christian concept of morality.

But even more, we tried to teach them that the door to God is through Jesus Christ, with all that implies; in other words, the basic tenets of the Christian faith: theology, if you will!

And if I could say anything to young parents just beginning the task of childrearing, it would be this: never let anyone convince you that your home and that you, as parents, are not the most important human factors in your child's growth and development. Think through your Christian beliefs. Establish your own strong relationship with your Lord, for you can never hope to guide your children effectively if you are hazy about the most important questions life poses.

And don't think your children will let you off easy: they can ask more profound questions than you can begin to answer unless you've done some deep pondering, studying and praying.

It's not easy. But along with the headaches, there are many marvelous moments and lots of fun.

And when you're finally cresting the hill and you see your children assuming the responsibilities of adulthood—well, you have to experience it to know how rewarding it is! ●

Families
Should LIVE
Together by Bruce Shelley

After 20 years of teaching college and career young people, I am convinced that many Christian parents need help in understanding today's youth. What are the major features of the youth outlook?

Most young men and women respond more readily to emotion than to reason. They are attracted to "happenings" rather than discussion of ideas. Dr. Richard W. Lyman, president of Stanford University, wrote in the *Stanford Observer* about the wave of anti-intellectualism that is threatening the United States. "Seldom has a glorification of instinct enjoyed a greater popularity than today," he said.

When a young person happens into one of our churches he is not as impressed by the pastor's well-reasoned arguments for Christianity's truthfulness as he is by church members enjoying Christianity.

Second, young people are more interested in personal freedom than in social order. They are more sensitive to their own liberties and to the needs of others than to the values of programs and institutions.

Many are irreverent in their attitudes toward the sanctity of marriage, premarital chastity, civil obedience, the accumulation of wealth, and the right or competence of parents, schools, and government to make decisions affecting their lives.

Pastors and churches which come across as inflexible authorities, interested primarily in adding numbers to rolls and dollars to budgets, are not attractive to many young people today.

Third, youth are in search of a mystical experience rather than material possessions. After growing up amid great economic uncertainty, parents determined to provide their children with the material comforts and pleasures they themselves were denied. As

54

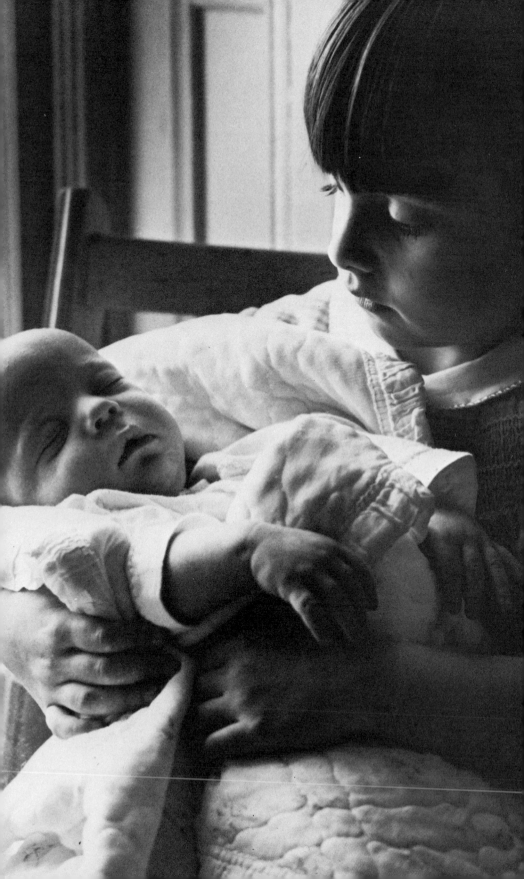

a result, many teenagers have been cushioned from economic shocks and cannot understand why their parents measure success by cars, clothes, and homes. Deprived of their parents' driving force in life (the struggle for things), youth have turned to drugs, sex, mysticism, sights, and sounds in the hope of directly touching reality.

This emotional, liberating, mystical quest often reveals a basic spiritual hunger. Who am I? How can I be accepted? What is life all about? How do I fit in? How can I find peace? These spiritual longings lie just beneath the surface of slogan-filled conversation.

How can concerned believers have an effective Christian influence on youth?

Sometimes I think Christian service, like charity, should begin at home. Much restlessness of today's young people is traced to conditions in yesterday's families.

A child's task is self-definition: "Who am I?" Growing up requires objects that he can push against in order to become stronger. He matures by testing himself against limits set by loving adults.

Study after study shows that two entities are vital to a child's independence. First, he requires warm, firm parents who love each other and on whom he can model himself while growing. Second, families must provide opportunities for the child to prove his competence in work and love. The Bible speaks directly, "Fathers, do not provoke your children to anger, but bring them up in the discipline and instruction of the Lord" (Eph. 6:4 RSV). Mature and responsible children are nearly always offspring of mature and responsible parents.

Parents should recognize that discipline comes from being a disciple. Both words originate from the Latin term for pupil. Children become disciples of parents who enjoy and back up one another. Mutual parental respect and praise for work well done allows a child to draw a positive self-image. In truly Christian families "no" is said as lovingly as "yes," and children learn to wait. Limits require reasons, but once firmly stated they must be enforced.

Positive factors in building disciple-families are time and listening. Parents and children should never stop doing meaningful activities together. Making a living is important, but it must never overshadow the process of raising children.

Generation gaps have been with us since Adam and Cain. There is nothing new in father and son differences. What is particularly acute in our time is a communication gap. Many parents have no idea what their teenagers think because their children are never given a chance to explain. "Can't you see I'm busy?" is a put-down that ought to be banned from the parental vocabulary. Educator Clark Kerr advises parents, "Spend time, not money." There is probably no better investment.

A large number of today's young men and women who need Christ have left homes they despise. It is too late to change their childhood, but not too late to provide an alternative family. That is the importance of a disciple-church, a family of God.

How can churches help today's youth? During the last four years as a professor at Conservative Baptist Theological Seminary, I have closely observed a significant ministry to college and career young people. I am convinced four things can be done for effective evangelism and church renewal.

First, introduce young men and women to Jesus as a *personal* Savior. Many searching for intimate person-to-person experiences find satisfaction in Christ—not a code or a creed, but a living Person. Jesus Christ said, "If anyone thirst let him come to *me* and drink." He is still inviting and still satisfying.

Second, provide young adults with a warm, small-group experience. Collegians are convinced the church is primarily a money-raising institution defending traditional values. They need to feel the warmth of a church that is primarily *people*. They need to see other Christians struggling, confessing, praying and caring. They need involvement in a church family that practices biblical standards and love.

Third, lead young believers from an emotional experience to a faith resting on the Scriptures. The youth I know come to Christ because of deeply felt needs which Jesus Christ often meets through some emotional crisis. Our task as more mature believers is to relate their experiences to the Word of God. The permanent stability of young believers depends upon our success in this effort.

Finally, provide opportunities for young people to serve Christ meaningfully. Paul says faith is "active in love" (Gal. 5:6, RSV). The current mood of activism among the youth can and ought to be directed toward Christian service. This is important not only for broken lives that need mending but for young believers themselves.

We must care enough to share our faith by word and example. Only then will understanding emerge in parent-child and adult-youth relationships. ●

Grandma
Had a Remedy by Rose M. Sloan

Values are as elusive as skittering crabs. They are hard to find, hard to see, and ever more difficult to pick up.

Our grandparents did not have that problem. If my grandmother had been asked what it meant to teach values, she would have answered without hesitation, "Teaching kids to do what's right!"

She had strict modes of behavior to achieve those aims. Children were expected to answer their elders with "no, ma'am" or "yes, sir."

"Teaches respect," Grandmother would have said.

If there were no chairs for guests, children offered theirs. They stood in the background, not daring to interrupt conversation. Guests were served first and children ate later.

"Teaches consideration," Grandmother would have said.

If caught misbehaving, it was the rod of punishment.

"Teaches obedience," Grandmother would have said.

Both the parent and the child accepted the unwritten laws governing behavior, each understanding the expectations and consequences of rebellion.

"Teaches them that there are certain ways to behave in society," Grandmother would have said proudly.

Fifty years later, I call Grandmother's methods harsh and stifling. Yet I want the same results. I want our children to be honest, respectful, considerate, obedient, and hardworking.

What are values? To me they are inner attitudes that determine how a person will react to the situation around him. Ever since we became Christians, my husband and I have searched out values and tried to implement them by trial and error. We want to instill in our children at least five qualities which are pleasing to God.

The first is a *glad heart*. Parents unanimously cherish a willing attitude. How it lifts the heart of a mom or dad when a child makes his bed after being reminded only once or does the dishes without making everyone else pay for it.

A parent must repeatedly reinforce a glad heart attitude, preferably starting when the child is small. If our daughter Carmen sets the table, we comment more on her willingness than on the beautiful table. If our son Carl picks up his toys without bringing us to the edge of our tempers, we comment more on his attitude than on the clean floor.

The second value is a *forgiving spirit*. What more ideal place is there for a child to learn forgiveness than within the family? Where else are there daily situations prime for explosions and trials?

Fighting between siblings can provide great opportunities to teach. After allowing time for the kids to cool off, we give each child a chance to explain his feelings while the other listens. It can be quite revealing for one child to find out how the other one feels.

Eight-year-old Carl was deeply hurt by his eleven-year-old sister's non-caring attitude toward him. "You say you're sorry and I take it, and you just do it again," he sobbed. "You just don't care!"

This had been going on for some time. To be honest, it seemed that Carl was right. One day, I sat down with them to talk about it. Deeper reasons for their quarreling became evident.

Carmen was feeling pressured to play with Carl. For years she had been his favorite playmate. They often had played pretend-games for hours. Now she no longer liked to play the same games. She preferred to play with girls her own age. Carl was losing a playmate and didn't understand it. Carmen felt resentful toward Carl, and she didn't understand either.

By listening to each other's feelings, Carmen was able to see how deeply hurt Carl was, and he began to see that Carmen was changing. He didn't particularly like it, but he became more accepting of her refusals to play. Both children forgave each other more readily once they understood the other's feelings.

The third value is *an attitude of thankfulness*. In our prayer times, we thank God for our food, our house, our health, and each other. We have all heard of the toddler who says, "Thank you for the spaghetti, the fork, and the spoon." It's cute, but it's more than that. The child is learning to be thankful.

Such an attitude is particularly helpful when a child is faced with hard times. During the fourth grade, Carmen was sick with an undiagnosed illness and missed a quarter of school. During that time, as we prayed each day, we were able to find something to be thankful for.

We were thankful for the excellent home teacher, the brief outings Carmen was able to take, the playmates who occasionally visited. We were thankful for the blessings that God brought out of it, such as her being ahead of her class when she went back to school and learning that God can provide comfort in hard times as well as good times.

A fourth value is *consideration for others*. Norm Wakefield, father of five and author of *You Can Have a Happier Family*, says, "If children do not grow to care about others and show this care in specific actions, they may develop into basically selfish persons. I cherish the wish that my children become persons who care deeply about others and act with compassion."

Consideration is taught in small ways, such as helping a toddler share his precious toy, encouraging a brother to think of his sister when he buys a candy bar, or thanking him for including her in his games when he has a friend over and she is alone. Acts of consideration often happen spontaneously. Notice and praise the child.

Children need to learn consideration for adults too. A friend of mine taught her small children to say "Excuse me, please," when they went to interrupt a conversation. Those few words acknowledge that it isn't just a child's world.

The fifth value is *self-worth*. Each child is unique and should be appreciated for that uniqueness.

We are quick to praise and admire those who have physical beauty or strength or height. How much better it would be to praise the inner qualities, to notice if a child is sensitive, or quick of mind, or loving, or creative, or enthusiastic. Then we could encourage each child's self-worth, regardless of his physical attributes.

Carmen has had a terrible time with spelling. In helping her to cope with her discouragement we remind her that God made her a unique person, different from anyone else. He gave her many abilities and gifts, but he didn't give her everything. She has a hard time with spelling, but she is good in reading.

A positive outlook also helps a child accept aspects about himself that he doesn't like. When Carmen developed freckles on her nose, her father started to count them. If he counted a certain number, he knew that she belonged to him. It was a funny little game, and her attitude toward the freckles remained casual.

Wakefield points out another important aspect of self-worth: "At our house," he says, "it means not comparing one child with another. . . . One excels in one area where another excels in another area."

In teaching these five values, we parents inevitably have to examine ourselves. Do we reflect a glad heart, a thankful attitude, a forgiving spirit, consideration for others, and a feeling of self-worth? We are passing our attitudes on to our children whether we realize it or not.

I think Grandmother would agree: we can focus on the inner attitudes that cause behavior as well as the behavior itself. ●

Blessed
Are the
Retarded by Dorothy L. Hampton

My only child is a little girl of nine. She is tall for her age and extraordinarily pretty, with large dark eyes that sometimes seem to look right through you.

So attractive is she that people have come to me in the supermarket and exclaimed over her—and then they have stopped mid-sentence, for it suddenly strikes them that she is different. And indeed she is. My little girl is mentally retarded. Her I.Q. is between 50 and 60, classing her with the trainable group of the retarded. I write therefore as the mother of a retardate, but more than that, as a mother who has put her heart and her life in Christ's hands.

Three out of every hundred persons are mentally retarded. This means that, in a state such as mine, one out of every eight persons is as closely related to a retardate as mother, father, sister, brother, uncle or aunt. Here is heartache. Only three percent of the mentally handicapped are institutionalized; the remaining 97 percent are at home, many of them without adequate schooling, recreation, friendship and church life. Some may say, "But I honestly don't know any retardates." Nevertheless they are with us—perhaps hidden, perhaps mildly retarded and "passing" in the community, but all needing the evangelical church and what it can offer.

There are several stages through which one goes upon learning that one's child is mentally handicapped. For those who do not know that Christ controls all that happens in their lives, there is usually a harrowing time of guilt and self-examination. Parents ask themselves again and again, "What did I do to give birth to such a grievously handicapped child?"

As a Christian I went through this for a mercifully short period, yet even with scripturally-grounded believers the psychological mechanism is not wholly cancelled. When a mentally handicapped

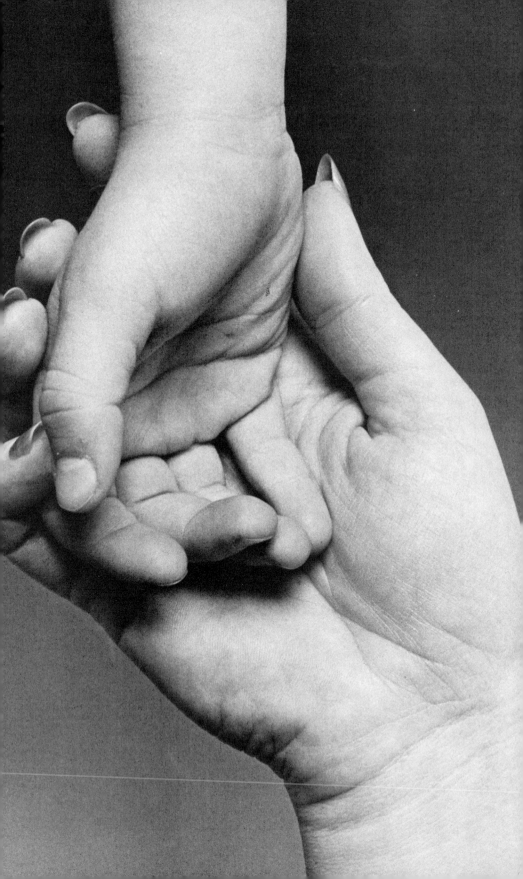

child is born, this mechanism may lead to bewildered questioning: "Lord, why me? How can I live with this? What shall I do?"

Some unfortunate parents never progress beyond this stage. To the great detriment of themselves and their handicapped child, to say nothing of any other children in the family, they remain preoccupied with "I", "me" and "us." Most parents of retardates, however, pass out of this stage to a second, in which their thinking is all directed toward the child involved. Here the normal reaction is to ask, "What can I do to help my child, only mine?" Hopefully, most parents pass into a third stage, that of asking, "What can I do to help all mentally handicapped children?" Only then, they realize, can they help their own child.

If my faith offered only some practical guides to everyday living, I would not be able to write this. But for Christians who have such inescapable problems, it means everything to know that we have a hereafter to count upon for us and our children. We have a God who is all-powerful, all-loving, and in control. We know that our children are provided for in God's eternal plan, that the incarnate God himself said, "Inasmuch as ye have done it unto one of the least of these, my brethren, ye have done it unto me" (Matthew 25:40).

All of us have a great deal to learn about the problem of retardation. Every retardate has parents and often brothers and sisters who desperately need Christian friendship, Christian love, a church home, and genuine acceptance. How sad to hear it said about church classes for the retarded, "Oh, they don't care. They won't do anything but sit in their ivory towers and criticize!"

Why is this true, not only concerning retardation, but also in respect to alcoholism, mental illness, and the underprivileged poor? Why are some evangelicals letting their liberal friends do works of compassion while they argue about immersion versus sprinkling and whether Christ will come before or after the tribulation—and all the time souls are perishing in the agony of despair over a mentally retarded child, an alcoholic or mentally sick relative? While Christians who have knowledge and understanding of the power that alone can save souls and ease burdens quibble over how separated they are, there is intense spiritual suffering going on in the very blocks where they live.

What should Christians do? Let me offer some suggestions based upon experience. First, they must realize that retarded children and adults need to feel wanted and that church life is important for them. "But," someone says, "their mentality in most cases limits their understanding of doctrine." Such a statement overlooks the wonder of the Gospel. Most retardates understand something about death; many can understand, to a limited degree, the concept of an all-powerful Being; many understand wrongdoing; virtually all can understand love—the quality they need more than any other. Thus many mentally retarded persons are able to understand something of the central truth that Jesus is God and that he loved them enough to die for them. This is the magnitude of the Gospel and its magnificent simplicity.

I believe that my child understands this great truth. Whether she is or ever will be at the age of discernment I may never know; but she loves Jesus, and she knows that he loves her. And if she could not grasp even this, I would still know that he loves her.

A teacher of a primary-level church class for normal children told me recently how a rather severely retarded child entered class the day the Gospel story was told. Instead of being a behavior problem as the teacher feared, the child sat very still. At the end of the lesson the teacher gave a simple invitation to accept Christ. The retarded child stood up, asking over and over, "Can I? Can I?" There were tears in the teacher's eyes as she said she knows our Lord is as happy over that little one as over any other.

Secondly, Christians must understand that it is not enough to say, "Let's have a church class or Sunday school class for the retarded." Every retardate has a family, and these are often in greater need than the retardate. What about the parents and others in the family? Is the teenaged brother of the little mongoloid made welcome and shown that his church understands? Does the congregation realize that mongolism is not hereditary and is not the result of some hidden sin of the parents? Evangelicals might well start group therapy classes for parents, never forgetting that the greatest therapy comes through personal knowledge of Christ as Savior and Lord.

Today in an inarticulate but eloquent plea the retarded are calling for help. It is to the lasting credit of the late President Kennedy, whose oldest sister is mentally retarded, that he heard that plea and led the movement resulting in the first legislation in America's national history designed to help the retarded.

Emotional response is not in itself sufficient. Response must be informed. This means that Christians must take the trouble to learn the difference between retardation and mental illness. They should know what facilities their communities offer for therapy and schooling for all retarded. They should be aware of the need for greater educational opportunities, more job openings, additional legislation in the field of retardation, and institutional reforms. They should find out what parents' groups are available where fathers and mothers of retardates can meet others with similar problems. Above all, they should know that retardation can happen to any family, that it is no respecter of education, social position or economic status.

Parents of retarded children can become victims of the most callous medical quackeries—money-draining schemes that claim miracle cures. The parents must be helped to realize that there is no cure. There can be great progress for the retarded child in some cases, nevertheless retardation is a condition, not an illness to be cured. Apparently our Lord meant for the retarded always to be with us, needing our help and understanding.

All children take their cues from their parents and the adults around them. Normal and gifted children must learn compassion for their unfortunate brothers or sisters. They should be told that handicapped children may be coming to church or Sunday school, that this is how God made these children, that they are to be helped and loved. Normal children will surprise parents and teachers with their matter-of-fact acceptance and willingness to help.

Many more professionally trained persons—teachers, medical researchers, therapists, recreation directors, counselors—are needed. So much can be done for the retarded, many of whom when trained and supervised are able to lead useful and happy lives. Here is a call to Christian service for youth. Such service entails more than professional skill, it can mean helping parents of retardates to a sure trust in Jesus Christ.

The young father and mother who have just been told that their baby is retarded can be given understanding and hope for eternity. While they cannot be offered immediate happiness, they can be shown that there are things more important than mere happiness.

Too long have most Christians lagged in assuming their burden for the unfortunate and the handicapped. We who have mentally retarded children need more than sympathy and tears. We need what committed Christians have to offer in knowledge of sins forgiven, in courage for living, and in a blessed hope for the future. Let Christians to whom much has been given give of themselves and of their bounty to help the unfortunate. Let them give in love.

We parents of the mentally retarded have heavy burdens. But when you free our souls by giving us the joyous knowledge that Christ is God, that he died for us and for our children, that he cares for us, that he loves the unlovely, that he is with us day by day, then there is nothing we will not strive to do for our children and all of "the least of these (Christ's) brethren." ●

Dear Dad and Mom by Elizabeth C. Jackson

Recently a college student candidly remarked, "Something must be wrong with me. My parents and I get along fine. I think they're great."

Unfortunately this somewhat humorous observation seems to contradict the parent-child relationships which are being discussed in our news media as well as in lectures, church groups and informal gatherings. Christian parents should have a distinct advantage in handling this problem, since they have not only the bond of the physical familial relationship but also a spiritual bond as members of the family of God. Yet frequently the relationship breaks down on both levels.

What is the crux of the problem? There is no simple analysis, no quick solution; but a few of the honest comments of college students might be helpful in alleviating the tensions and fears experienced by many families. Christian college students are sincerely trying to communicate with their parents. What are they saying?

"Love me—I need you."

In discussing a problem she was experiencing with her parents, a young woman said, "I have tremendous respect and love for my parents and I know they deeply love me, but I've never really 'felt' their love and I'm very lonely for it. I need them."

The personal need for genuinely warm and responsive love is greatly aggravated and accentuated by the depersonalizing processes of this age. The need for a sense of belonging to a loving family group, often unfulfilled, has driven many young people into undesirable personal involvements.

Parental love expressed in intimate, thoughtful care is basic to the security and well-being of a child. He never outgrows the need to "feel" the love of his parents. Love for God is more easily understood

and experienced by those children whose parents have communicated love, concern and understanding in the home.

A child who has no sense of loving involvement at home, no family loyalty, finds it difficult to understand the concept of loyalty and service to God based on love and worship. Often a confused, searching young person must be "loved" to God, and the only kind of love he can understand at that point in life is one that expresses sincere concern, a love that notices and cares about the little things, a love he can "feel."

"Respect me—I am an individual."

One reason many students are rebelling is their need for identity, individuality and respect. They react against the old rubber-stamp process, even though the end product of their desire for nonconformity often appears to be nothing more than a new kind of conformity to things which are mysteriously important to them.

Christ was a nonconformist to the Pharisaical rubber-stamp establishment of his day, but more, he was a Man of God identified as a true individual who conformed wholly to the will of his Father. Young people can understand this concept and respond to the call of Christ in these terms. They are not asking for an easy Christian life; on the contrary, they are searching for an individualized relationship with a personal God.

Today's Christian youth seem to realize that God has indeed created all men equal but not alike. They are different in desires, tastes, personality traits, gifts, capacity and potential. They sense that God wants them to develop their individuality according to his will and for his glory. They are to be wholly surrendered, totally committed and Spirit-controlled—but still distant, one-of-a-kind persons who deserve respect even though they differ from every other member of the family. A Christian young person wants to be himself for the glory of God, and he wants to be respected for his faith in God even though he expresses it in new terms.

"Trust me—I must learn to make my own decisions."

In general the well-adjusted college students are those whose parents have carefully entrusted them with the responsibility of developing values, weighing judgments and making personal decisions. It is impossible to prevent a child from making any mistakes. These are inevitable and a necessary part of the development and maturing of the individual.

Overprotective parents slow down the process and sometimes permanently stunt the development. There is no better place for a young person to grow than in the understanding environment of a Christian home or college. Here there are those who care and understand, who trust and pray, those who can pick up the pieces, put them together again and send the fledgling on his way with fresh confidence based in a new reliance on God.

Young people ask for guidance, but want the kind that is coupled with confidence and is free of suspicion. They want to be taken at face value, respected and trusted, realizing all the time that they will probably make some stupid blunders and foolish mistakes but knowing their parents will understand they must learn to make decisions. Young people can and will accept guidance and correction, and even discipline, when they know that they are trusted. Often young Christians have serious difficulty in trusting God because they have never been trusted by their parents and do not understand what this relationship implies.

"Accept **me**—*even though at the moment you can't agree with my ideas."*

A sense of personal rejection by their family often alienates young people from their home and church. They do not actually expect their parents to agree unreservedly with all their new ideas (often they are not wholly convinced themselves), but they want and desperately need the sense of basic acceptance as a person, as a dearly loved member of the family regardless of open disagreement on many issues. Everyone still needs to "belong," and a sense of rejection will only frustrate and even produce bitterness.

Young people can accept constructive, honest criticism when it comes from one who is standing by them, identifying with them in a deep love relationship. They are aware that their temporary search is leading them into new areas which are frightening to their parents (they are frightened too), but this is one of the ways they learn to find themselves in God—to know him and trust him. Differences will come, but these must not disturb the deep consciousness of mutual love and acceptance.

"Forgive me—and then let's forget it."

"I don't dare ask my parents to forgive me—they'll never let me forget it." This is the matter-of-fact comment of many Christian young people.

Frequently parents wonder why their children do not come to them in the hour of failure and defeat. Perhaps they are afraid. Parents who express understanding and trust in their children are, at the same time, making themselves approachable so that in the time of failure their children will feel free to turn to them. This is the perfect time to prove the love and loyalty which are often difficult for parents to express overtly. Frank discussion, wholesome criticism and constructive discipline are all essential parts of the parents' responsibility, but the patient, gracious, forgiving spirit of Christ is what brings healing to the wound. After all, did not Jesus say something about "until seventy times seven?"

"Listen to me—maybe I have a good idea."

College students are thinking seriously and they want to be heard. They are asking parents to listen—listen—listen. The sacrifice of one hour's time spent in attentive listening may mean more to a student than the sacrifice of Dad's paycheck. Talking things out is amazingly therapeutic to the young person and helps him to objectify his problem. Often he can find his own solution as he verbalizes a complex situation to an understanding listener. As for the older generation, listening often proves to be instructive and at times inspiring.

Young ideas are fresh and vigorous. Young minds find new ways to approach old problems, new terms for expressing old ideas and new figures for worn-out clichés. New terms do not necessarily change old principles—and perhaps a contemporary term is far more meaningful than an old one. Although sometimes lacking in maturity and experience, young people are presenting many good ideas which are shaping the world of the future. Listen!

"Be honest with me—tell it like it is."

Much of the criticism about double standards is tragically true. The present Christian community can benefit greatly from the direct questioning of modern youth as they frankly point out blind spots and challenge outdated methods. How can their questioning be resented if it is done with honesty and with Christian courtesy?

These Christian young people love God and the church; they are anxious to be involved in meaningful service for God. It is time to face up to inconsistencies, irrelevancies and inadequacies in both the Christian home and the church. Young people see these issues very clearly and their respect and loyalty can be gained by honestly facing them together and then, with God's help, making necessary changes.

Christian youth today are demanding a Christian faith that is "for real." They are much more willing to bear the rugged cross than most of the Christian community realizes. We do not need to drape the cross with a garland of flowers. Let us give it to them as it is. There are still those who will respond to the privilege of suffering for Christ.

"Teach me of Christ—by your everyday life."

An attractive college girl recently paid her mother the supreme compliment when she said, "My mother is the best Christian I have ever known." Parental precepts are meaningful only when they are substantiated by an exemplary Christian life in the home.

Modern audio-visual techniques frequently used in public schools have served to make young people keenly aware of their environment, more perceptive in drawing conclusions. In short, they are looking for a Christian example which is audio-visual—an example in which they can "hear" and "see" Christ. They are looking for honest, open, genuine Christians who make living for Christ the most important business in their life. It must be "for real" and it must relate to the total pattern of life—to the needs of the whole person. They look for Christ first in their Christian homes.

College life brings about many changes in the student, but it need not estrange him from his parents. In fact, this is the very thing he does not really want to happen. Although the geographical separation seems to be intensified by the rapid development in his ideas, attitudes and behavior, the ties of family love should be maturing and growing stronger as God's blessing and guidance continue to rest on the Christian home. ●

"Yes, I Said No!" by Rosalyn Hart Finch

"**I** have to see that movie, Mom. Please! All my friends say it's really tough."

"No!" I said for the third time. Trying not to look at my visiting friend whose silent disapproval hung heavy in the air, I excused myself and my youngster from the room.

In the kitchen out of earshot, I repeated my negative answer to my offspring, this time in triplicate, "No, no, no! End of discussion and/or argument regarding X-rated movies." Weary of hashing over the same old scene, I added, "Do not bring up the subject again."

Back in the living room, I was irritated with myself for feeling guilty, as if I owed my guest an explanation for daring to cross my insistent child.

On every side people are asking: What is happening to our moral standards? Why is dishonesty becoming so commonplace? Why are children so hard to manage these days? Perhaps one reason is our mass reluctance to use (and back up) one of the shortest but most effective words in the English language: *no!*

Of course it is good to be affirmative and positive. America was built on the power of positive attitudes and actions. But if life is to be successful in every sense of the word, a positive attitude needs to be tempered with common "horse sense." Nice as it would be to live in a world where hope and joy abound and where sin and immorality are nonexistent, we must be realistic, too.

To say "Yes" or even whisper "Maybe" to crime, dishonesty, and immoral behavior is unthinkable. To say nothing is even more dangerous. We must be willing to say a loud, resounding "No!" to some things and then be ready to do whatever is necessary to back up our position.

Many Americans are not saying no when they should. Many of

us are befuddled. We are wringing our hands about our moral climate, but are doing little to change it.

Parents often shy away from saying no for fear their children won't like them. Even though authorities tell us our offspring are actually begging for discipline, we hesitate to provide it lest we incur their displeasure.

We actually support a great deal of disgusting entertainment because we provide funds for our children to attend it. A very loud "No" is needed in this area.

As voters we often elect (either by voting without knowledge or by *not* voting) politicians who make promises they can't carry out. We can register our desire for clean politics and good moral government by our concerned interest and our votes.

As avid readers of a great variety of literature, we spend millions of dollars annually on books and magazines that contain much immoral material.

A strong "No" rejecting such pseudo-sophisticated material would get much trash off the market.

Our ancestors gave us so much with which to build a good life in this country. With their tears, sweat, and blood, plus God's blessing, they fought wilderness, drought, sickness, poverty, and sin to build a tremendous nation for future Americans. They would not understand how, through our lack of moral courage, we have allowed this country to slide to its present state of decadence.

Those of us who desire to see our beloved country strong must begin to say no when it needs saying—and it should be said firmly, not timorously.

We will have to say no sometimes to our own temptations and self-indulgences, even if we risk being labeled square or old fashioned.

When we say no to our children who ignorantly or innocently ask for undesirable things which they consider necessary to be "with it," naturally they won't like it. But somehow we must help them swing away from demanding more and more while putting forth less and less effort, or future generations can already be counted lost.

A definite "No" now and then could do wonders for those parents and children who have ceased to find each other credible.

Let's stop being the silent majority and start saying a strong "No!" to the wrongs of society.

Let's become actively indignant about racial prejudices and injustices, but let it be said with love and backed up with action. ●

Parents in Pain by John White

"**H**oney, a police car just pulled in front of the house."

Jim and Elaine stared at it, ominous even without flashing lights. A couple of bystanders stopped to watch along with some neighborhood children. Curtains across the street were slowly drawn aside.

For a minute nothing happened.

Then from the car emerged two uniformed city police officers. One of them held the door open to allow a bedraggled youth to get out.

"*Peter!*" Elaine said hoarsely. Yet she was not surprised. She had long feared this very scene.

Slowly Peter, his head held high and defiant, walked up the path between the two officers. Jim and Elaine felt suspended in a foreign universe. Yet when the trio finally reached the front door, the bell sounded with unnatural clarity.

"Oh, God!" Elaine said softly. "What do we do now?"

Some parents don't care. They've learned to live with it or to shrug it off. But thousands, perhaps millions, are being torn. Their pain is the worse because many of them have a need to cover their tragedy. Appearances are more important to some parents than to others. You notice that church dignitaries and political figures tend to hide their family tragedies, facing the world behind masks.

Are you a parent in pain? I cannot promise to heal you, but there is ease in sharing pain. Many parents have shared with me. Some have written their stories and allowed me to relate them in these pages. Names and certain facts have been changed to protect their privacy. But the essentials remain that others might be comforted.

My object in writing is to come to the rescue of parents. It is only

incidentally to deal with child rearing. Books on how to bring up children from birth through college are ten a penny. Yet all the books on child rearing have not stopped the flood of adolescent problems and tragedies. What is needed is something to help parents in anguish to grapple with their distresses and to find hope in their despair.

Although I am a practicing psychiatrist, my confidence does not spring from any psychiatric expertise. For I am also a practicing father, one who has made mistakes, who has struggled at times with a sense of hopeless inadequacy and who has grappled with the shame and the pain about one of his five children, who went astray. I have known a sickening dread when police cars drew up to my house and men in blue walked up the path to the front door. I have known wakeful nights, rages, bitterness, frustration, shame, futile hopes being shattered, and the cruel battle between tenderness and contempt.

Lorrie and I had no idea what we were in for when we got married. We *thought* we were aware that family life would never be a bed of roses. I was proud about entertaining no preconceived notions on how to bring up children and that I never criticized other people's child-rearing practices. I was not going to have anything to unlearn when I became a parent. Yet neither of us anticipated the long series of jolts and joys, ecstasies and agonies that awaited us. My "open-mindedness" was full of delusions, of false expectations, and of unproved assumptions.

As Christians, we talked about our total inability to run our lives apart from God, and we thought we understood what we were saying. Christ would be at the center of *our* marriage. At the same time, with pious naiveté I imagined that such an intelligent, spiritual husband with such a beautiful wife would undoubtedly give rise to four children (we planned four but the last one turned out to be twins) who would be the envy of parents everywhere.

As matters turned out, it was Lorrie and I who were startled. As the years passed we grew progressively more humiliated and hurt. We little foresaw the day when we would sit in mutual pain, both of us silent because we had nothing left to say.

But if we had our lives to live over again we would not have it different. For in months and years of darkness we learned lessons we could never have learned in the light. Our souls have been stretched so that they now have a capacity for both joy and suffering that they never had before. The pain that could have shriveled and embittered us has made us stronger, more alive.

We have found God in a way and to a degree we never did before. We have found that he too is a parent who is willing to share the secrets of all parenting, who in fact invented the very institution. He knows more than the experts. In him we found healing and peace. By him we learned day by day how to cope with impossible problems. Through him our marriage is more solid than ever. He taught us what praying for our children was all about, what we could pray and what we couldn't.

We still are learning and we have more learning to do. But we would be selfish to keep our joys and solace to ourselves. They need to be shared as widely as possible. I write about them with the prayer that they will heal parents in pain, and if it shall so please God, restore many of their children, however impossible the situation might seem right now.

Where did I go wrong? Am I still doing things wrong? Am I to blame? Such questions haunt many a parent.

These are crippling questions. They can make you tremble inwardly with anxiety and self-doubt. Instead of setting you free, they impede your footsteps on an icy sludge of uncertainty, rendering you ineffective and indecisive. You become a pathetic victim of fears—fears of doing the wrong thing, fears of the future, fears of more problems, more pain.

But let's begin at the beginning. Did you go wrong? Certainly you have made mistakes. Every parent has. But are you to blame *for what has happened?*

It could be. But it is doubtful that *all* the blame rests on you. Unhappily, the questions which look so simple are in fact complex. We may consult whatever authority we care to and the unhappy fact remains. Yet consult we must. I propose to look at three: common sense, science, and the Bible. Each has something to suggest, though my personal bias (surprising, perhaps, in a psychiatrist) is to rely mostly on the Bible. Nevertheless, all three keep offering us their suggestions—common sense and science a little more pushily than the Bible. Let us turn to them first, reserving a discussion of the Bible for the next chapter.

I have known several families during my life where the parents were a disaster—quarreling, drinking, neglecting the children, running around, partying, separating, divorcing, whatever. Yet their children turned out well. That is to say, they did well at school, got jobs, seemed to have decent friends and now appear to have stable marriages in which they handle their own children sensibly. If you talk to the children, as I have done, they all say, "I swore that my home would never be like my parents' home," or, "I saw what booze did in my family, and I swore I'd never touch it," or, "I was the oldest. I knew what it was like to have to look after my kid brothers and sisters night after night. My kids are never going to suffer that way."

I am also acquainted with families in which the parents are warm, firm, wise, yet giving—and who have at least one child in serious trouble. Some of the parents are nonreligious, others religious, including sincere Jews, Catholics, and Protestants.

On the other hand we have also seen that parenting does make a difference. I checked recently on ten children in serious trouble in our area (this isn't science we're dealing with now but common sense) to find that nine of the ten came from broken homes, and all ten from homes where parenting was shocking by any standards.

In other words, there are general rules. Good parents are less likely to produce problem-children than bad parents. Stable homes are more likely to produce stable children than unstable homes. But that's as far as it seems to go. There are no steel-reinforced rules which say: good parenting always produces good children; bad parenting always produces bad children.

When doubts and anxieties assail us, common sense is the first thing to go. We long for easy answers, unambiguous assurance. The doubts and guilts drown our minds and make us not *want* to think rationally, but instead to cling to any bit of ideological driftwood that comes along. The last thing we want to do when we are drowning is to think logically.

Yet think we must.

I don't know where you may be as you read these words: a parent fearing the future, a parent relaxing a little after the crisis, or one in the midst of one. But I must insist on this ground rule: at times *force yourself to think* even when you may not feel like it.

Which brings us back to where we started—common sense. Whether you are a Christian or not, you will need plenty of it in dealing with yourself, your family, and the child who causes you so much pain. And I say again that common sense says that all the blame does not necessarily lie with you if one of your children goes badly wrong. It may. But it's rarely so simple.

The same turns out to be the case when we turn to science. Obviously we cannot in a few words cover psychology, sociology, anthropology, ethology, genetics, systems theory, epidemiology, neurophysiology, and biochemistry, all of which are among the branches of science that are concerned with the question: Why do people turn out the way they do? Fortunately, all we need to do is to note one or two obvious things.

As we look, not at one branch, but at several branches of science, we discover that they are not greatly in conflict with one another so much as preoccupied with different areas of the same subject. The findings of the main branches of the human sciences, for example, anthropology and psychology, are more frequently complementary than they are contradictory.

Anthropology looks at the influence of the culture in which children are reared and notes the correlations between tribal customs and beliefs and the particular characteristics adults display. Margaret Mead, for instance, describes two tribes in one area and their different characteristics. One tribe was hostile and aggressive, another very peaceful and gentle. Mead attributes the differences to child-rearing practices in the two tribes.

If we turn to the psychologies, of which in the West the two most influential seem to be the various learning theories (behaviorism) and psychoanalysis, we find that they take a close-up of why people turn out the way they do.

The different schools of psychoanalysis are concerned with what goes on inside growing children in response to their relationships with parents, brothers and sisters, and "significant others" impinging on their development up to adulthood. Learning theorists are primarily concerned with the way our central nervous system responds to its environment. They theorize about the mechanics of

84

how children and their immediate environment interact to affect their behavior and what we might call their personalities.

The area of study is very similar in both schools. Though there are fundamental theoretical differences between the two, both have marshaled evidence in an attempt to show that what happens to children as they grow determines how they will turn out in the end. Moreover, both offer some hope of change for the better where things have gone wrong.

Unhappily, the claims they make to help people may be exaggerated. No school of psychology can help someone who refuses help. And this is precisely the problem you may face when your child has gone badly wrong.

Anthropologists and sociologists confirm the powerful influence of rapid social change, of mass communication, and peer-group pressure on growing children. Unlike primitive tribes where family and culture are homogeneous, in our case clashing cultural influences often compete with the home. We are fools to ignore their power.

There was a time when people who believed in heredity and people who believed in environment quarreled fiercely about which of the two was responsible for Sue's piano-playing talent. "She had proper training from an early age, and she idealized her dad [a concert pianist]," one person might say. Such an explanation attributed Sue's flair to environment, the home environment that shaped her early years. Others will say, "It's in the family. They've been musical for generations. It's in their blood." In so saying, they declare themselves on the side of heredity.

In science this became known as the nature/nurture controversy. Few scientists today quarrel about nature versus nurture. Some of us may have a tendency to attach more importance to one part than to the other, but most of us agree that both play their part. We speak of "genetic loading" regarding mental breakdowns, illnesses such as schizophrenia, and some forms of depression. We recognize that some people have more of an inborn tendency to these things than do others.

Genes may not merely be the conveyers of brown eyes, straight teeth, and wavy black hair, but of subtle character traits. Our children are shaped not only by the atmosphere in our homes but by the combination of sperm and ovum that united to give them their physical, mental, and emotional potential. And as parents we had no control of either the genes we passed on or of how they interacted when conception took place.

The main thrust of my argument could be summarized as follows: it ain't that simple. There are too many factors involved for us to be able to assess each one accurately.

But what about a problem child? Did he have no real say? Did he merely *feel* as though he were making choices? Is he nothing more than the sum of the influences that were brought to bear on him? Or is he something more? As a Christian I believe we can never "explain" John scientifically. John is John. He has a will. He chooses. He is pursuing a path he himself selected.

Neither we nor our children are entirely free. Yet neither are we helpless slaves. At times we may groan with St. Paul, "Wretched man that I am! Who will deliver me from this body of death?" (Rom. 7:24). At others we will realize what William Ernest Henley was trying to say when he wrote, "I am the master of my fate; I am the captain of my soul."

Careful thinking tells us that we can neither take all the credit for our children when they turn out well nor all the blame when they turn out badly. Genes, home environment, school and social environment, and the child's capacity to make certain choices all bear on the final outcome.

Nancy was a Christian worker we knew who developed breast cancer when she was pregnant with her second baby. The baby survived. Surgeons removed Nancy's breast and radiologists treated her. The surgeons told her that her chances of living long were poor since the cancer had developed at a time when her breast tissue was at the height of its activity—preparing to secrete milk.

Nancy prayed. Her husband Jon prayed. Lots of us (we were part of the same team) prayed. People in churches prayed. Some prayed for healing, others for grace to accept whatever God might send.

The story is too long to tell in detail. Over a year passed before Nancy eventually died, and during that year she, Jon, and several other people were convinced on the basis of the Bible and the Holy Spirit's assurance that God had granted Nancy supernatural healing.

There could be no doubt of Jon and Nancy's faith. Certain passages of the Bible seemed to come to them with special force. Nancy was happy, rejoicing in the wonder of God's goodness. She seemed oblivious to her slow, erratic downward course as flesh dropped from her bones and her skin hung loosely on her. Even her deep pain was dismissed as arising from other causes. Jon assured me God had told him, suddenly as he one day knelt in the barn to pray, that he need have no fear: the healing was complete.

For some people I have known, dashed hope based on a mistaken faith has had more traumatic consequences than unlooked-for bereavement. Their relationship with God has been shaken. If you have been mistaken in trusting God for healing, how do you know that you are not mistaken in a lot of other areas? A good shake-up can startle us into seeing truth.

Many parents get hurt because they find false hope in the Bible. I do not mean that the Bible is unreliable, but that in their concern for their children, parents may read the Bible through magic spectacles. Parents are not alone in this tendency. All of us in trouble are inclined to do the same.

If you are a parent grieving over a child who has gone wrong, you may have to abandon false faith as a first step to finding real faith. You may have been reading into the Bible things that are not there.

Many Protestants along with Orthodox Jews count on certain promises in the Bible. The most quoted one is in the book of Proverbs: "Instruct a child in the way he should go, and when he grows old he will not leave it" (Prov. 22:6, JB). The words are taken as a promise made by God to any parent who rears his or her child in God's ways. Such a child will continue to walk in those ways as he grows older. And since God never welshes on his promises, it follows that parents of an erring child may do one of two things. On the one hand they may say, "We brought our daughter up well. Therefore, although things seem very black at the moment, we may count on the promise of God. Sooner or later our girl will return to what she was taught so well when she was a child." In this way they may derive comfort from the promise. On the other hand, they may see her delinquency as evidence that they failed as parents, in which case the promise becomes an accusation.

A prime rule you must follow in interpreting the Bible is to take into account the context in which you find a given sentence. What about Proverbs 22:6? If you examine its context you will discover that the verse is not a promise made by God to anybody. It is a statement, a *general* statement about how family relationships normally work.

The book of Proverbs is part of what is known as the "wisdom tradition" in Hebrew thought. Unlike the prophetic tradition in which God's messages (of comfort, denunciation, and specific future predictions) are proclaimed to God's people by his prophets, the wisdom literature consists of inspired observations and reflections on daily living by wise and godly men. The sentence, "Instruct a child in the way he should go, and when he grows old he will not leave it," is such an observation. It tells us what we can see all around us if only we open our eyes. Good parents usually produce good children.

"Aha," people say to me. "But you're adding a word. You're saying 'usually' and the verse doesn't say that!" True. Neither does it say "invariably." It's not that sort of verse. When we interpret it as an inflexible law, we are reading into it something the Holy Spirit never intended.

Why am I so sure of this? Because the book as a whole makes no sense otherwise. It is a book which presents both sides of the coin: good parenting promotes godliness; disobedient sons are heading for tragedy. It points to examples we can see anywhere, in any culture, in any age. They include observations about disobedient children as well as of good and bad parents. They are divinely inspired observations. It is not their spiritual source that I am calling into question, only the proper way of understanding them.

Parents are admonished to bring up children properly. Children are admonished to respond wisely to parental correction. If both play their part all will be well. But it takes a parent-child team working in harmony to produce this happy result. Good parenting is part, perhaps the major part of the story; but a great deal of emphasis is placed on attentive, obedient children who listen and welcome the correction of their parents.

God created a world in which Adam himself could choose the folly of disobedience; it must surely follow that the godliest and wisest parents can never guarantee wisdom or godliness in their children. God has given no promise that they ever will be able to. As one parent put it without any bitterness, "You are not just trying to raise your child. You have had to take a piece of damaged goods and are trying to restore it. Sometimes this is much harder."

We may teach; we may admonish; we may train; we may discipline; we may love. But unless in the case of a child we see him or her as much more than an extension of ourselves, we have not begun to learn what life is all about.

In a moment of terrible despair and grief, have you ever wished that he or she might conveniently die or disappear? How many times have you cried, "I just cannot take any more?" Perhaps your pain and shame may have been made worse by the fact that you had yet to learn the most basic rule of all. You cannot ever control another human being, even if that human being is your own child. You do not have the right to. You may discipline and teach; you may train; you may point the right course; you may "shape behavior patterns"; you may reason; you may plead. But you cannot and may not ever control.

When should a parent seek professional help for a daughter or son who creates problems? How can a parent decide what sort of help is needed and who is best qualified to give it? Should a Christian ever seek help from a non-Christian? Don't the Scriptures contain all the wisdom I need? Isn't it really compromising (sort of "going down to Egypt") to consult a professional? Will I be showing lack of faith by doing so?

Let us be clear what we are asking. What do we need? Obviously one doesn't ask a plumber for advice on gardening or a musician to diagnose cancer. Nor would one normally consult a pastor about the color scheme in the living room or a Sunday-school teacher about an investment portfolio.

Matters may not be so clear, of course. If God is an expert on everything, presumably we should need no help from other experts. But God is not a substitute encyclopedia. Who looks to God for information the yellow pages were designed to give? Who prays for directions to find Brown Street when there is a city map in the glove compartment? Who, for that matter, prays for their thirst to be quenched when a faucet lies at hand? Why seek from God a cure for weariness when a bed is waiting and the hour to get into it has arrived? God is not a Celestial Convenience. He has provided us with normal means, and in our relationship with him we shall make little progress if we fail to use them.

But God and the Scriptures deal with moral and spiritual issues. How can we consult a psychologist if the problem is basically one of righteousness and faith? Will not the psychologist smile condescendingly and tell us there is no problem?

Obviously, professionals vary, not only in their faith but in their capacity to help. Some are warm, others cold. Some are wise and experienced, others green and silly. Some are so tied to theory that they view all problems through the spectacles of their ideological prejudices. Others hold theories lightly because they are keenly aware that problems and people do not always fit into little boxes. Some are pompous and conceited, others gentle and compassionate. In short, they are human beings.

Even in matters of faith there is no black and white. There are crooked, incompetent Christians whose primary interest is in making a fast buck or playing the big shot. There are competent, courteous non-Christians who, though they may know less about the Scriptures than you do, will from their wide experience be able to offer solid help in areas you have never thought about.

Experts in counseling are no different from experts in any other area. They are technicians, technicians in human behavior, perhaps even in brain mechanisms and bodily functions. We all know stealing is wrong, but sometimes experts can put their finger on the reason that stealing is a special temptation to Herman. In the same way, we all know that children should not dodge homework. But psychologists can sometimes identify special difficulties Carol has with symbols, the reason for her distractability.

Christian parents may see only the *moral* aspect of a problem. Professionals, while not ignoring the moral aspect, can identify the psychological aspect which may or may not be of importance. In the case of some of my patients it can be of very great importance.

Nicki, age sixteen, was subject to bursts of rage at school and at home. He talked incessantly, laughed hilariously at times, slept only four hours every night, was overactive, and got into fist fights constantly. Seen by a psychiatrist who specialized in problems of adolescence, he was diagnosed as hypomanic. On a small dose of lithium carbonate (an inert salt) his excessive talking and activity were reduced to normal, and his rages, his inappropriate laughter, and fighting all disappeared. Rages and fighting have moral, psychological, and physical aspects. Nicki's psychiatrist detected a physical disturbance underlying the outbursts. Once this was regulated, Nicki's temptation to give way to fighting and bursts of rage was dramatically reduced.

Let us look at some serious problems in teenagers that call for professional help and then, having done so, discuss varieties of counselors and their usefulness.

1. *Pregnancy.* Few things shake parents so much as pregnancy in a teenage daughter. Mos parents assume that an illegitimate pregnancy is something that only happens in other families.

A number of options face the girl and her parents. The pregnancy can be interrupted. It may be allowed to go to term and the baby be adopted at birth through an agency. It may, on the other hand, be adopted by the girl's own parents, or she may keep the baby herself. Finally, the father of the child may marry the girl, in which case the couple could generally keep the baby.

The implications both of keeping the baby and of allowing it to be adopted should be discussed fully and frankly by everyone concerned. Finally, whatever decision is reached must not be made *for* the pregnant daughter. Though the temptation to take command will be great, especially because of the tendency to overcompensate for failure to keep your daughter out of trouble, you must resist it. The decision needs to be made *with* her and *by* her.

2. *Alcoholism.* You should suspect your son or daughter has a major alcohol problem if he or she has been drunk on several occasions over a period of a year or more. Definitions of alcoholism are unsatisfactory. Perhaps the best and simplest is that alcoholics are those who have lost control of their drinking and who by drinking are damaging themselves socially, physically, or otherwise. Thus if your child's drinking has been associated with delinquent behavior on several occasions, you should suspect alcoholism.

Face your son or daughter with the possibility that he or she has an alcohol problem. Make it quite clear that an alcoholic is not someone who is down and out but simply someone who gets into trouble with drinking. Make it clear, too, that there is nothing you, the parent, can do to solve the problem. The only solution is for him or her to renounce alcohol for life. Otherwise it may slowly gain complete mastery in his or her life.

You may not be sure of the seriousness of the problem. Most social workers, psychologists, psychiatrists, and counselors are competent to assess and give an opinion on the matter.

Psychotherapy and counseling have almost universally proved unavailing for alcoholism. Most experienced therapists would agree that while it may or may not be true that certain psychological problems underlie alcoholism, it proves futile in practice to try to solve those problems until the alcoholic has stopped drinking.

The expense and the value of treatment programs vary widely. It is wise to find out all you can about any institution before you suggest that your teenager avail him or herself of the treatment. AA (Alcoholics Anonymous) groups are usually not suitable for adolescents who feel out of place among older men and women. Alateens sometimes is helpful for them, even though its aim is to help adolescents cope with drinking parents.

You will notice that I said *suggest*. My reason for doing so is that universal experience has demonstrated that someone with an alcohol problem must *want* help before help can be effective.

3. *Homosexuality.* To discover your child is involved in homosexual practices will come as a terrible jolt. But hold steady. If you are to help your child, panic and rage should be allowed to subside before you talk.

Your child may or may not want help. He or she may not even want to discuss the issue. If this is the case, there is little you can do. The longer the practice has continued, the less likely it is that your child will want to quit. Some homosexuals can be helped to reorient their homosexuality if they desire help. With others the reorientation is extremely difficult. If your child is willing, it may be helpful to consult an experienced psychiatrist or psychologist.

If you want to get a glimpse of the inside of the mind of a homosexual, I suggest you read Alex Davidson's *The Returns of Love* (InterVarsity Press), a sensitive and moving account of the struggles of one Christian homosexual.

4. *Mental illness.* Almost inevitably when a child's behavior is bizarre and inexplicable, parents will turn anxiously to a psychiatrist. Dreaded terms like insanity, nervous breakdown, schizophrenia begin to suggest themselves.

Mental illness poses at least three kinds of problems for Christian parents. The first concerns the future. As frightening changes take place in the way their child thinks, talks, behaves, and as the child they once knew and loved turns into a stranger, they begin to ask, "What does the future hold? How will this end? Will our child ever be able to earn a living?"

Mental illness is no more and no less related to sin and to demonic activity than are cancer, diabetes, or pneumonia. Some illnesses are the direct result of sin. Injuries from car accidents may result from drunken driving, and brain syphilis from sexual promiscuity. More commonly the relation is indirect. We are vulnerable to sickness (mental and physical) because we are fallen sons and daughters of a fallen Adam and Eve. It is just as appropriate to seek medical help for psychiatric illness as it is to do so for asthma or rheumatism or ulcers.

The term *counselor* is gradually becoming an umbrella term covering everything from those who give intensive psychotherapy to others who offer gentle advice. Because the training of counselors varies widely, their skills will likewise vary, some having special skills that others lack. Psychiatrists and psychologists, for example, will have a better working knowledge of the central nervous system than pastoral counselors whose expertise lies in biblical and doctrinal knowledge.

There are thus two kinds of information one should seek about counselors: first, about their training and theoretical orientation, and second, about their personality. Both kinds of information are important, and if one kind is more important than the other, I would say (though many professional colleagues would disagree with me) that it is their personalities, their length of experience, their degree of interest in each client, their capacity for warmth, their objectivity and freedom from prejudice.

1. *Pastors.* Some pastors give time to counseling even though they have had no special training. Others take special courses from seminaries or from seminaries in conjunction with university behavioral

93

science departments. Their training may include a theoretical review of different psychological schools along with some practical supervision of clients they counsel during their training. It may lead to a doctoral degree and even postdoctoral work. Usually the training places special emphasis on marital and premarital counseling. Some pastoral counselors are trained to administer psychological tests to people they seek to help.

2. *Psychologists.* Psychologists are specialists in human behavior whose primary interest is in normal rather than abnormal behavior. Many psychologists devote themselves to research, studying animals to gain clues about human behavior or else studying undergraduates, the species of human they have the greatest access to. They could be referred to as *non-clinical* psychologists.

Other psychologists are trained to administer tests, tests that attempt to evaluate personality, intelligence, and potential problem areas. Increasing numbers of psychologists are interested in counseling which they may refer to as psychotherapy. Nowadays *psychotherapy* can mean whatever the user of the term wants it to mean and is often used synonymously with counseling. Christian psychologists who have thought carefully about psychological theories in relation to a biblical view of human nature are in a position to make use of the insights from various schools without adopting the underlying philosophies associated with them.

3. *Psychiatrists.* Psychiatrists are physicians who have specialized in mental illness. Unlike psychologists they have a greater tendency to focus on abnormal rather than normal behavior. As a psychiatrist myself, I believe our greatest usefulness lies in the diagnosis and the treatment of the graver forms of emotional disturbance. However, psychiatrists vary as much in interests, activities, and beliefs as do psychologists.

4. *Social workers.* Social workers, too, whose role used to be conceived as that of giving direction to people whose distress called for social help, are now increasingly engaged in general and marital counseling and psychotherapy. Their training may include both theoretical and clinical exposure to psychological theories and to counseling practice.

5. *Nonprofessional groups.* It should be clear by now that while I have a healthy regard for good training and proper qualifications

I have an even greater respect for experience, intuitive perceptiveness, and a capacity for warmth. This being the case I would not hesitate at times to recommend the help of nonprofessional agencies.

The people who will help you most may in fact be parents who still struggle.

Many years ago when I worked in a bank, our early morning ritual consisted of meeting before the massive doors of the strong room. Five of us each had a different key so that only when all of us were present could we gain access to the strong room. The absence of any one of us seriously hampered the day's work. Let those of us then who are troubled seek one another out. Alone, our progress may be hampered by rigid doors of steel. But the same doors may yield in moments when we bring our different skills and insights to share with one another.

There are no courses in parenting. Books can tell you what to do, but doing it is another matter. It takes the lifetime of at least one child to learn to cope with the full range of that child's reactions. And the learning you do on one child is by no means guaranteed to be suitable for the next. If between child needs and parent capacities there is a gap, what is the godly attitude to adopt? Let me suggest a few principles.

Concentrate on your assets. Take stock. Make a list of your strengths and weaknesses, but let your focus first be on your strengths. Check the list with your mate or any friend in whom you have confidence. They may see some strengths and abilities you may be unaware of.

Don't be too influenced by magazine stereotypes of an ideal parent. Take your list and thank God for what you have. Some of your strong points may seem to have no potential for helping your children. No matter. Thank God for all he has given you. Praise him as the true source of your assets, all of which come from him.

Never pretend to your children that you are better than you are. Let them know you are a fellow struggler, one who may have known glorious victories but equally ignominious defeats. Don't pretend to be victorious if you are not. I do not say you are to bare your soul to your children, or to reveal to them the horrors of every pit into which you have descended. But where your conduct in the home has been blameworthy, be open about it. And be open about God's grace to you as well. They must not see in you a paragon of virtue

95

but a redeemed sinner, one who goes on learning and who refuses to be discouraged by falls. Give them someone to follow, not someone to worship.

Don't brood over your failures. Yes, your sins and weaknesses have harmed your children, just as your parents' weaknesses harmed you (and just as your children's weaknesses will damage their children, from generation to generation). We do not yet live in the New Earth. The curse, though no longer triumphant, still has power to sting.

But brooding over the damage you have inflicted on your children will help nobody—least of all your children. It is good to recognize your faults. It is better to confess them, yet without morbidity or self-pity but with straightforward honesty to God and to your children.

The curse still operates in family relationships. But the redemptive power of Jesus Christ operates where your failures have damaged and go on damaging your children. I do not altogether know how this is so. But I know that no insights are so profound and no liberations so triumphant as those where grace touches the scars and brokenness that come to us by sinful inheritance. And in every weakness your children were born with and in every psychic wound your own sin has inflicted on them lie seeds of miraculous grace. Water those seeds with your prayers, and you may one day worship as you see godly strengths and glories spring forth from the very bruises inflicted by sin.

Many books have been written about child discipline, both by Christians and non-Christians, but none that I know deals adequately with the issue of punishment. Discipline is generally seen as enlightened and good, punishment as old-fashioned and bad. Parents who think in terms of punishment may be labeled *punitive*, a term synonymous with *hostile, vindictive, vengeful* and *cruel*. Perhaps it is time we reexamined the place of punishment and exercised greater caution before jettisoning such ideas as blame and guilt. None of us wants to defend punitiveness (at least in the sense in which the word is commonly used). But punishment can be administered by patient and merciful people. It is not necessarily the invention of "punitive" people, nor are those who give it necessarily being cruel.

96

The aim of discipline is to train the person being disciplined. Discipline is a means by which that person's behavior may be shaped to please the rest of us and hopefully in a way that will be better for the person receiving the discipline. If a child has the habit of stealing, for example, discipline will aim to make him or her more honest.

Punishment on the other hand aims to rectify an injustice. The person being punished is seen as guilty of a wrong. He or she owes a moral debt to the rest of us. The punishment is viewed as a means of putting the wrong right, repaying the debt, and removing the guilt. "You deserved that," a parent might tell a child who is being punished. "I have paid my debt to society," says the criminal who emerges from jail.

Thus whereas discipline aims to help the person disciplined, punishment aims to benefit society, both by meeting its demand that evil not pass unrecognized and by serving as a warning to all would-be wrong-doers. If punishment does anything for the wrongdoer, it will give him or her the sense that "now my wrong is paid for and I can forget about it."

B. F. Skinner, both in fiction and expository prose, has boldly outlined a scheme to bring about a world order of peace by using what I have called the treatment model. Skinner does not see people as made in the image of God. Indeed one of his books is entitled *Beyond Human Dignity*. Without thinking, many Christians have opted for a Skinnerian approach to child raising. Because they are Christians, they subscribe theoretically to the idea of human dignity, of the dignity of their children, but fail to see the inconsistency between their faith and their child-rearing methods. Yet in divorcing discipline from punishment they join forces with Skinner. Such parents shape behavior patterns, exterminating undesirable traits, conditioning and deconditioning. The more closely they follow certain child-rearing manuals (be those manuals "Christian" or not), the more they become concerned with the "end product," a convenient "end product" that will fit more comfortably into family life, church life, and society in general.

They have unwittingly fallen into error. They have ruled out mercy and have adopted principles inimical to human dignity. Skinner freely recognizes this. You cannot mold someone's character and behavior without regarding that someone as a *something*. You have gone beyond human dignity into a Skinnerian world.

Happily, our children resist our best efforts to fit them into molds. They wriggle and they struggle until the behavioral molds crack and splinter. They may not know what dignity is, but its presence in them cries out to be heard. The dignity that God placed there will defy our attempts until we are compelled to see the image of God in the little ones we try to shape to our pleasure.

Few divine attributes move us more than a display of God's mercy. Mercy awakens awe in us. It awakens our desire to worship and appeals to that which is most noble in our characters. It can have the same effect on our children.

Training and discipline alone do not allow for mercy. It is not merciful of a dentist to ignore a decayed tooth and send a child home. It is not merciful of a coach to excuse a top athlete from a critical part of training. In the same way, to adopt exclusively a therapeutic approach to child rearing rules out the practice of mercy as well as of punishment.

How shall our children learn mercy unless it is shown to them? How shall they learn that wrong deserves punishment unless they are not only disciplined but punished? How shall we as parents accord our children the dignity of true humanity unless we teach them that their moral wrong merits punishment and that punishment in some ways rights the wrong they have committed? How shall we teach them the sinfulness of sin if we treat it as a bad habit we can train them out of? Punishment may teach a child to quit sinning, but it should be given if it is truly merited whether or not it will make the child quit. And in considering whether a child deserves punishment, we shall hopefully think long and hard before deciding on a just sentence.

Yet I suspect our children really do not need to be taught that sin is sinful. They already know. It is we, their parents, who have frustrated ourselves and added to our pain by struggling vainly to shape bad behavior, having failed to see it as sin that called for either retribution or grace.

How are we to view God's terrible judgment on his people, especially on the vanished Israelites from the northern kingdom? We know that he is not a cold and inscrutable judge. However exact his judgments, he remains a God of love.

Yet love must respect the dignity, the personhood of the beloved. You cannot love someone truly and deny that person the dignity of facing the results of his or her decisions. To do anything else would be to betray true love for something less than love, a "love" tainted by selfishness and weakness.

The father of the prodigal son let his son go. And God the Father of us all does likewise. He who could coerce our wills refuses to. There is a limit even to his pleading. He does not block the doorway as we try to leave him, flooding us with a thousand arguments. Nor does he pursue us, pestering us with, "I told you so." He gives us the full dignity of choice.

There is wisdom as well as justice in what he fails to do. There are times when our wills are so set on disastrous courses that disaster alone will teach us. There is nothing like a belly full of husks to teach a man that he's a fool.

But as parents we are selfish in our loves. We cannot let go. We refuse to see what stares us in the face, that a heart set on folly will not be dissuaded by reason.

Habits are hard to break. "She just *will not* learn," we tell ourselves in frustration, having gone over the lesson with an obstinate daughter for the hundredth time. The habit of correcting her has grown to be so much a part of us. As the time draws closer for her to live her own life, we correct her all the more fiercely. We are scared by what we see awaiting her. And in our terror we become the more diligent to avert tragedy and attempt to teach the unheeded lesson for the hundred-and-first time. We cannot believe our own words, that she just will *not* learn!

It is not love that makes us so persistent, but fear. The time has come for relinquishment, and we lack both the love for our child and the trust in God to relinquish the battle of wills. Growth into adulthood demands the continual exercise of choice. In adolescent years our children vacillate between an innate drive to become independent from us and the habit of childhood to cling to us dependently. The nearer they get to adulthood, the greater becomes the drive for independence. And independence implies learning to trust one's own judgment. You cannot make real choices without running real perils. And we cannot defend our children from the perils of their own choices.

Do not feel guilty about allowing your children to reap what they have sown, for this is how God deals with all of us. He does not enjoy letting us pursue our stubborn way until we live with pigs, but faced with a choice between giving us the full dignity of personhood with all its attendant risks or enslaving us to involuntary servitude like the beasts, he chooses the former. He could not make us a little lower than the angels without facing the possibility that we might choose to become little better than demons. Love says, "I will give you the high dignity of choice, even though you choose to fling my gift back in my face."

Clearly, letting go is a matter of degree, and the degree to which I let go will increase over the years. In fact, our hand may often be forced by realities which wrest control from us. Yet if we adopt an attitude of relinquishment, we may save ourselves and our children some needless frustration. Moreover, we will be giving our children the same high dignity that God gives us.

You will notice that there is a difference between God's standards of parenting and human standards. His are infinitely more stringent. Nevertheless his demands are less grievous.

If you follow human standards, the way is open both to pride and to despair since there is an implied cause-effect relationship between your performance and the results. On the one hand it can make you unjustifiably proud, for your children may grow up respectably *in spite of your poor parental performance.* On the other hand, if your children go badly astray in spite of conscientious parenting, you take all the blame and are given no way out.

Make it the aim of your life to adopt God's standard and leave the results of doing so with him. Bring him your loaves and fishes, telling him it is all you have, but look at what he demands you do with the loaves and fishes. It is not your responsibility to make sure 5,000 stomachs are filled. It is your responsibility to obey instructions. Beside the Sea of Galilee, it meant to go on breaking and passing bread as long as the supply lasted. As a parent of growing children, it means that you will go on striving to be to your children all that God is to you. It is God's part to look after the miracles.

In your own pain and tragedy, you are being invited to enter into a close relationship with God. Whatever may or may not happen to your children, great good and enormous enrichment can come into your own life if only you will draw near to God. You may not receive unusual experiences or glory in visions, but your spirit can be set free. You can pass through fire and come out as fine gold. You can become more truly alive, more aware. Your very pain brings with it the possibility of untold riches. ●

Love Begins at Home by Ruth Graham

France, according to a statement I came across in a woman's magazine, has had 69 kings, only three of whom were loved by their subjects. The article went on to claim that these three were the only kings who had been brought up by their own mothers. The rest had all been reared by regents, tutors and governesses.

A short time after finding this statement, I read in a magazine a discussion of "Discipline: Strict or Permissive." Numerous quotations were given from surveys of children and the ways they respond to their home environment, social environment, and life in general.

The interesting conclusion of these surveys was that it did not seem to make too much difference whether a child was reared in strict surroundings or permissive discipline, or whether brought up "by the book" or "without the book." What formed the child's character primarily was the overall atmosphere of the home, especially the attitude of the mother in that home.

That women have far-reaching influence no one will deny, but just how far-reaching only eternity will reveal. But along with this influence will come almost overwhelming responsibilities and pressures. Taylor Caldwell wrote a column in an American journal recently entitled, "Women Get a Dirty Deal."

I read this column with great interest. The author quotes an Oriental woman friend of hers, who claimed that the American woman is more put upon, more abused, and more mistreated than any woman on the face of the earth. Well, this was a switch to me. I thought that we were a tremendously privileged group, but when I had finished reading I began to feel sorry for myself.

It seems that we are expected to be chauffeurs, cooks, shoppers, housekeepers, mothers, wives, plumbers, cleaning men, yard-men—and so the list goes on *ad infinitum*. I began to wonder that

102

there are not more female alcoholics, more women trying to escape from their lot through barbiturates and psychiatric treatment and even through suicide.

I could not help thinking of an old Southern caretaker at a hunting lodge in Georgia. Friends of ours who own this lodge spend weekends there frequently. Each evening, as was their custom, the men gathered for Bible reading and prayer before retiring. One night they asked Ram, the caretaker, if he would lead in prayer. He commenced by saying, "O Lord, have mercy on us, 'cause mercy suits our case." After reading Miss Caldwell's article, I had the same feeling: "Lord, have mercy on us, for mercy suits our case."

Sometimes I feel that life does not tend so much to crush us as to distract us from the main purpose of being wives and mothers. I recall that on the Graham farm in North Carolina there was a cow dog in-the-making that showed tremendous promise. Whenever he was out rounding up the herd he performed magnificently—until a butterfly or a bird flew across his path. Immediately he was off, head up, ears flapping, tail wagging, barking furiously. He went through all the motions of being a good cow dog but for what?

Sometimes I think that we go through all the motions of being good wives and mothers, and yet what are we doing? "Mercy suits our case." And God has been merciful, for in Jesus Christ we have the solution to our problems. In Him we see God revealed.

A friend of ours told us about her brother who had gone overseas during World War II, and a month or two later his little daughter was born. She was a toddler before he was able to return. The family gathered to watch the father become acquainted with his daughter for the first time, but all were heartsick when she would have nothing to do with him. "But I'm your daddy," he would say, whereupon she pushed him away and ran to the desk where sat the large portrait of her father. "No," she announced, "that's my daddy."

For several days this went on, and the family had to blink back the tears as they watched the young father trying to make friends with his wee daughter. One evening he knelt on the floor to play with her, and she looked intently into his face, then ran over to the desk and studied the portrait carefully. She flew to her mother, clapping her hands, and cried out, "Oh, Mommy, they're both the same daddy!"

It is impossible for us to read the Gospel of John and to study the rest of the New Testament without realizing that Jesus Christ is God Himself. Not only is He God revealed, but He is an example to us.

If you study the Gospels you will discover that our Lord was the eldest of at least seven children. We are given the names of Jesus, James, Joseph, Judah and Simon, besides at least two sisters. Joseph must have died when Jesus was still a youth, for he is not mentioned after the episode in the Temple. Thus Jesus was left the chief bread-winner for a family of seven children and a widowed mother.

For me this is deeply significant, for there is not a problem which we, as mothers, face, that He did not understand—particularly we who have to bring up a family for the most part alone. Our Lord knows the problem of limited finance, of overcrowded housing. He knows the tension caused by scrapping between brothers and sisters. He knows about teenage romances. He knows all the burdens that His mother carried.

I think it is rather sweet that at the marriage at Cana in Galilee, when the wedding guests ran out of wine, immediately His mother turned to Jesus. That indicated that she was accustomed to taking her problems to Him. I like to think that no matter what the problem is that I am facing at home, He knows about it firsthand.

Yet the fact that Jesus is our example can be very disturbing, for the more we see of Him, the more we see God revealed in Him, and the more there grows this sense of sin. Call it by whatever name you will, there is in each of us a sense of guilt, and if we do not deal with it, it can become a guilt complex. Psychiatrists face this daily: people who are trying to cope with their guilt complexes and are unable to do so.

I couldn't cope with my own. I remember when I first realized that it wasn't the quantity of sin that damns a person, it was the fact of sin. I prayed for forgiveness and I felt unforgiven; and the heavens seemed drab and the future was black. Then one day a friend suggested that I take the 53rd chapter of the book of Isaiah and put my name in it.

When I read that He was wounded for Ruth's transgressions, He was bruised for Ruth's iniquities, the chastisement of Ruth's peace was upon Him, and with His stripes Ruth was healed, I realized that when Jesus Christ died on the Cross, He died as my substitute.

But He did not leave us there. He did not desert us to grope through this life the best way we could. He said, "Lo, I am with you alway, even unto the end of the world." He is not only our example. He is our companion.

I cannot tell you what a comfort it is at home when problems mount, when one's husband is away or is occupied with world problems and other matters beyond the home, to know that Jesus Christ Himself is there constantly.

It is impossible sometimes for a busy wife and mother to get on her knees often. But to know that you can stand washing dishes, you can iron, you can clean, you can grocery shop, you can drive, and in whatever you have to do, Jesus Christ is there beside you, urging you to talk over your problems with Him—that is a joy and a comfort it is impossible to describe.

Last but not least, in Jesus Christ we have an advocate. The Scriptures tell us that He ever lives to make intercession for us. I don't know what problem you are undergoing, or what you have to face, but He does, and He is praying for you right now.

I think that is a significant point on which to close. Remember that we do not do all of the praying. We do pray, yes, and it is important that we do; but at the same time Jesus Christ Himself is in heaven praying for us; praying for you, praying for me.   ●

Growing Up Happy by Ardyth Stull

Some might say that I had an ideal childhood. My parents loved me and taught me to love others. I always had plenty of friends. I enjoyed school and I always liked my teachers.

I was also very active in the church: children's choirs . . . Bible school . . . youth fellowship . . . I was an acolyte . . . and I played the piano for Sunday school.

By the time I reached eighth grade, though, my happy childhood was a thing of the past. My rose-colored glasses had been yanked away from me; I was beginning to see the pain and cruelty of the "real world." I was still a "good" person, but I became an *unhappy* person.

In order to compensate for the emptiness that I was experiencing, I decided to get involved in more activities. So I became a cheerleader. I was in two school choirs and a mixed ensemble. I was an editor of our school newspaper. Yet, the more things I did the emptier I felt.

Another source of distress to me was my older brother, Mark. I had never felt that God was very fair when he was giving out gifts to my brothers and me. He gave to Mark all the brains. My younger brother, Paul, received a wonderful sense of humor. All I got was straight teeth!

Mark loves to read. When he was in third grade he was reading tenth-grade-level books. He quickly became bored with the books that kids his own age were reading, so he began reading some books that really messed him up. Mark grew increasingly rebellious and argumentative. He argued simply for the fun of arguing. His favorite sport was to take what anyone said and twist it around to make his victim look like a fool. One of his favorite playgrounds was Sunday school.

This made me furious. More than once I told Mark to shut up right in the middle of a Sunday school lesson.

When Mark announced that he was going to leave the church and become a Hindu, that was the last straw. This time I would show Mark that he was wrong!

While looking through some magazines of my grandfather's one day I found my ammunition. In a copy of *Look* was an article titled, "The Jesus Movement Is Upon Us." The article told how a revival among youth had started in California and was sweeping the country.

I thought surely Mark would change his mind when he saw that other young people were turning to God. Some of them even looked kind of freaky—I figured Mark would really go for that!

I took the magazines home and marched upstairs to his bedroom. I waved it in his face and said, "See, Mark? Don't you want to be a Christian? Everyone is doing it."

Within three minutes he had completely demolished me. No, he *didn't* want to be a Christian. No. He *didn't* want to rejoin the church. He could be just as good a person by being a Hindu as a Christian.

Feeling like a fool, I turned and ran out the door and down the stairs to my bedroom. For what seemed like forever I sobbed and sobbed. I felt so empty! For all these years I had believed in God but now, after a three-minute debate, I wasn't sure. I wasn't sure of anything.

My mother heard me crying and came into my room. She was afraid that I was sick.

I was sick all right. Heartsick.

I told mother (between chokes and blowing my nose) everything that had happened. I don't remember any of what she said to me that night. All I remember is that before she left she put her arms around my shoulders and prayed for both Mark and me. Her prayer soothed me.

Several weeks later my former church youth leaders decided to have a weekend retreat at their home. They invited youth from our church and also some students from nearby Kenyon College.

Mark and I decided to go. I wanted to have fun and Mark wanted to argue and mess things up for everyone.

On the first night of the retreat, several of the girls got together to talk with two of the girls from Kenyon. The college students told us what Jesus Christ meant to them and what he was doing in their lives. Before we disbanded to go to bed, they asked us to pray with them.

I knew that when someone was praying I was supposed to close my eyes, bow my head, and be very reverent. But when these two students prayed, I gawked at them with my mouth wide open. Their prayers seemed so personal! They looked so happy! I had never seen anything like it before.

In all the years that I had gone to church, no one had ever told me that I could know Jesus Christ personally. I had heard much about God as Creator and about love and being a good person. But knowing Jesus personally and letting him control my life? All this was new to me.

The next afternoon during a rap session I saw one of my friends, Jean, go upstairs. I don't know why, but I followed her. She was with Karen, one of the college students. By the time I got there Jean had asked Jesus into her life and both the girls were crying together for joy. I stood in the doorway feeling kind of silly. Karen asked me if I wanted to ask Jesus into my life, too.

I nodded and sat down on the bare wooden floor. Karen put her arms around my shoulders and began praying. All I said was, "Jesus, if you are really real and if you really do love me like these people say, then please come into my life right now."

I guess that was all I needed to say, because Jesus came in and he has never left!

I found myself sobbing as hard as I had just a few weeks earlier. But this time the tears were happy tears.

I flew down the stairs and told everyone what had happened. There was hugging and singing and dancing. All the other kids from the church asked Jesus into their lives that afternoon—all except Mark.

I went over to Mark, who was slumped on a couch. "Mark, don't you want to ask Jesus into your life, too?"

"Yes, I want it more than anything I've ever wanted before." But for some reason he couldn't quite surrender. Not yet.

That night we all went to a place called Chi Rho House where a lot of other Christians were fellowshipping together. And there Mark gave himself to God.

108

I was so happy I thought I would burst! I went over to Mark and for the first time that I could remember, we hugged each other. Only Jesus could have made that moment possible. ●

"O God–Not Another Baby!" by Beebe Carol

The regret, the guilt, the anguish are over now—transformed by God's loving nearness. But it all came back to me recently at a family reunion when a cousin, obviously expecting another baby, told me: "I only wish I could be as graceful about this baby as you were about Ronnie." And as soon as I got the opportunity I had to tell her the awful truth: I hadn't wanted Ronnie at all. In fact, I wondered if I could survive this "blessed event." How small my faith was!

Bob and I were disgusted when I went for my regular checkup and discovered I was pregnant—just two weeks after buying our much-needed new car. How could we afford a baby the same year? Also, we knew that Kim and Kelly would be ready for college before this baby started to school. We thought the baby would stretch our budget to the breaking point.

But looking back, I don't think the financial problems upset me as much as the emotional and time angles. I was already torn in so many directions: with one child begging for a new formal; one failing math; one needing braces on her teeth; and one still wetting the bed—I couldn't stand another baby!

Time-wise, I was working over 30 hours every week at home, plus keeping house, cooking, sewing, trying to be a good mother, and helping Bob in his work. I didn't have enough time to do things I already struggled with—how would I manage with a new child?

I just didn't want that baby, and neither did Bob. I felt sorrier for myself than him, though, because he was still trim and not sick. *He* didn't have to fight nausea every time he stood up too suddenly or smelled bacon cooking or stayed in a stuffy room too long. And *he* wasn't as tired in the morning as he was at night. I was angry with Bob and vice versa. We've been close in our marriage, but we stopped communicating. I guess we blamed one another like a couple of kids, but we were desperate.

110

Yet we both knew and loved the Lord. We've been used to lead others to himself. We've helped others through trials and tribulations. God had seen us through deaths and births before, but we seemed at a loss for help then.

I couldn't discuss my feelings with anyone, but I missed my husband's closeness most of all. I felt I was robbing my whole family of so much when the danger arose of a miscarriage the first three months, ruining our plans for a vacation we'd dreamed about for years. The doctor didn't want me to go; all the clothes I'd made for the trip didn't fit anymore; and the money we'd saved would have to pay the doctor and hospital bill.

You've never seen anybody as sorry for herself as I was!

"Me." That was the key word to my feelings. All my thoughts were centered on myself, not on Christ. But we never considered abortion because we feel it's wrong to take another life, even before it's born. So there was nothing to do but wait.

I suppose the turning point was one particular visit I made to my doctor. I was nearly four months pregnant then. Physically, I felt some better. The danger of miscarriage wasn't over, but the doctor told me I could go on the long trip. I had bought material and made three "Sunday" dresses and two at-home outfits which lasted the rest of the pregnancy.

Emotionally, I didn't feel one way or the other by then. I was going to have a baby. I couldn't do anything about it, so I simply tried not to think too far ahead.

But that particular day at the doctor's office, the nurse remarked, "Well, since you didn't plan on this baby, the Lord must have had a special purpose in sending it to you."

I couldn't shake off her words. She didn't know it, but she had struck a responsive chord. That night I searched the Scriptures for examples of "miracle babies." I hadn't thought of it before, but, suddenly, our baby did seem like a miracle baby!

I read about Isaac, Samuel, Joseph, and John the Baptist. And, of course, I read about the Lord Jesus Christ, too, the greatest miracle baby of them all. Job 1:21 came to my mind, too, although I'd never heard it used in connection with birth: "The Lord gave, and the Lord hath taken away; blessed be the name of the Lord."

No scientist can create life. Only God gives life. And God had created the life stirring in my body.

111

I couldn't understand why God would send us a fifth child when some of our friends longed for just one. But God isn't obligated to explain his will to us.

God had been speaking to Bob, too, for he came home one day and said, "Isn't it wonderful to think what God might have in store for this child?"

Our attitudes didn't change suddenly, but we found ourselves planning for the baby. We talked about a name and I began looking forward to the baby's ticklish kicks and punches.

Then when Ronnie was born I cried and cried, nearly hysterical. But my doctor assured us that all mothers react this way when they reject a baby at first. I was exceptionally tired, too, because Ronnie was born right at Christmas time. There in the hospital room, I asked God to remove all guilt I had carried because I hadn't wanted the baby at first.

I had expected to forget my extra work for at least a year, but when Ronnie was three weeks old I was working at home parttime. In six weeks I was working 30 hours a week again.

From the first, Ronnie never kept us up at night. So God supplied the rest I needed by sending an unusual baby. He's been a delight from the beginning, so lovable and affectionate. Ronnie has always enjoyed a good schedule. Even now, he likes to eat and go to bed by himself with a bottle or with his toys.

Now, I realize how much Tippie needed a playmate as he has enjoyed his little brother. The older children are so proud of Ronnie. They compete for his attention every day and he thinks they're the grandest people in the world.

And this last baby is a real daddy's boy. One of the first words he learned was "tie." He puts every string he can find around his neck and says "tie." His daddy thinks that is great! Bob's mother says Ronnie is the first grandchild who looks just like his daddy did as a baby. Also, he's the first grandchild who's been a grandmama's baby, too!

And another special blessing is that my own mother who recently went home to be with the Lord enjoyed three glorious weeks with Ronnie last summer. He was her last grandchild and a much beloved one because he would play in his playpen and entertain her while she was bedridden.

I've been a better mother and a better Christian since Ronnie was born because I reached the point of total commitment to the Lord. I had to accept the fact that my life is in his hands. There are problems and situations I cannot handle. I need the Lord every moment of my life. And once I realized this I grew spiritually. I learned to trust him—and to praise him—no matter what my circumstances are.

Ronnie is 18 months old now. Through the Lord's strength, I've been able to accomplish more these 18 months than I had hoped to accomplish in five years. God has opened doors for me and given me blessings that would never have been mine if I hadn't learned to lean completely on him. Through my unplanned pregnancy, God broke and remade my will.

Believe me, on Mother's Day I'll think about all five of our children and thank God for each one. But if I can get Ronnie still long enough, I'll hug him especially close to me and tell the Lord a special "thank-you" for the baby we want so very much. ●

"Forgive Me, I Was Wrong" by Ruth Hayward

Shopping with a neighbor, I waited as she was paying for a purchase, when suddenly she cried, "Oh!"

"What's the matter, Jean?" I asked. "Forget your wallet? I have enough to lend—"

"Oh, no, it isn't that." She drew out a bill and handed it to the salesclerk. "It's these. Cindy's gloves. She didn't have them to wear to school this morning. When I accused her of being careless and scolded her for losing them, she told me she had given them to me after Sunday school yesterday. I didn't believe her."

"That's all right," I said, "just tell her when she comes home from school."

"Tell her? Indeed not. I don't want her to think her mother is so forgetful."

"But, Jean, she has a right to know that it wasn't her fault."

Jean looked at me sternly. "Children have the right to look up to their parents as good examples—not as imperfect blunderers."

I protested again. "But we are *not* perfect."

"Why admit it, Ruth? After all, there is such a thing as pride."

I did not say any more on the subject. So blundering at times in my own family relationships, I had no right to preach to my friend. But I still do not believe pride has any place in family relationships, whether between parent and child or man and wife.

No matter how perfect we want to appear to our children, we simply are not. In spite of all our good intentions, we do blunder. We are mistaken at times in our interpretation of children's behavior. Sometimes we discipline unfairly.

I remember a time when my daughter, Wendy, had to stay after school because she had not handed in her homework.

114

When she came home I scolded her.

"But I did my work, Mommy," she declared. "I just couldn't find it to hand it in."

"Wendy—"

"But I did. Please believe me."

I went on. "Didn't you look at TV quite a long time last night?"

"Yes, Mommy. But I did my work first," she insisted.

Knowing she would not deliberately tell an untruth, I did not press further. But I was sure she had forgotten.

Later that night I was picking up some papers on the coffee table. I had been working on household accounts the night before and had left my work there. Now, sorting things, I came across a piece of notebook paper. Heading it was the name "Wendy Hayward," then the title "Science." It was the missing homework.

I picked up the paper. My heart pricked as I realized how mistaken I had been. I hadn't accused Wendy of not doing the work, but I knew that was what she thought.

Hurrying to her room, I noticed she was turned to the wall. Hoping she was not yet asleep, I called softly, "Wendy?"

She turned over. In the dim light I could see she had been crying, for tears still glistened on her cheeks.

"I found your homework, dear," I said.

She sat right up. "Now do you believe me?"

Taking her in my arms, I said, "Of course I believe you. And it was very wrong to even make you think I didn't."

"But that's all right, because it turned out right. I should have put it right in my notebook, but I was in too much of a hurry to watch TV. Next time I'll do better."

"And so will I," I promised.

When I was first married, I made the mistake that so many young people make. I thought all quarrels and misunderstandings were the fault of my husband. Quite often, though, it was proved that *I* was the one at fault, but pride kept me from saying so. Being young, too, my husband had the same attitude.

But one night he came to me, his arms outstretched, saying, "Ruth, I'm sorry. It was all my fault."

Taken by surprise, I found all the anger and self-righteousness drained from me, and I said spontaneously, "I'm sorry too. It was mostly my own fault."

115

That moment was a revelation to me. It made me realize we were not as incompatible as I had often thought. It made me realize that my husband was a reasonable, loving, understanding person. Most important, when I was not too proud to say, "I'm sorry," I made our life together much smoother and more rewarding.

And so it has been with our children. Conflicts between us have usually been when I, as mother, have been mistaken and failed to admit it. False pride, based on a natural desire to be regarded as an ideal mother, has, at times, kept a barrier between a child and myself much longer than was necessary. When I have "swallowed my pride" and admitted I was wrong, I have found an immediate, tender forgiveness and understanding from my very youngest to the oldest. ●

Children Deserve Chores! by Jack Eicholz

A middle-aged neighbor of ours was mowing his front lawn when he suddenly began to experience chest pains and shortness of breath, possible symptoms of a heart attack. His wife rushed into the backyard where their 16-year-old son was sleeping on a chair lounge and directed the boy to drive his father to a nearby hospital.

"Why wasn't your son mowing the lawn?" a neighbor asked the wife after her husband had returned from the hospital, well, but with orders to take it easy for awhile.

"I don't know," she replied. "We can't seem to get him to do anything around the house."

Those of us who had watched David grow from the toddler stage thought we knew the answer. He had never been taught to work. In fact, there were many occasions when he had been discouraged from doing chores around the house with comments like, "You won't be able to do it right," or "I can do it quicker myself."

Have you ever observed a five- or six-year-old, eager to help his daddy wash and wax the car, being chased away by a parent who is anxious to get the job done? When a child whose desire to help is dealt with in this way, it is easy to understand why he rebels later at a chore.

Social workers point out that the work a child does is not as important as the sense of responsibility he acquires. A youngster who is not introduced to work during the formative years may have trouble establishing a proper relationship with society as he matures.

The child's own attitude will often be the clue to his readiness for home jobs. This fact was brought home to a friend of ours, who was constantly a target for the question, "What can I do?" from her five-year-old daughter. To help solve the problem, she bought her enough toys for three little girls. A week later, as the little girl sat

117

surrounded by toys, she asked: "What can I do?" Toys are desirable for recreation and as educational tools, but many youngsters outgrow them early and begin to want to work with Mommy and Daddy.

At an early age, of course, youngsters seldom do a perfect job, and they also tend to lose interest quickly. But parents who exercise patience with these early efforts will find the teaching much easier as the child grows older.

In this age of mechanization and modern appliances, finding jobs that children of various age levels can handle is not always simple, especially for the city dweller. But the thoughtful parent can find many chores their children can and should handle. Here are some:

Preschool age: put away toys, empty wastebaskets, bring in mail, sweep porch, run errands in home, put away papers and magazines.

Grade-school age: set up or clear the table, wash or wipe dishes, iron flatwork, wash windows (inside), make beds, rake leaves, shovel light snow, use vacuum cleaner.

High-school age: put up storm windows, help with younger children, mow lawn, shovel heavy snow, paint, make simple home repairs, mend clothes, prepare entire meal.

When more than one child is involved, it is important that jobs be evenly distributed so that one youngster is not doing the more unpleasant chores every day or week. To help solve this problem when our own children were younger, we drew up a list of jobs for everyone, including ourselves, and pinned the duty roster on the family bulletin board. An extra column was provided so that we could check off each job as it was completed.

Some of the jobs, such as dusting, emptying garbage, and feeding the cat, required daily output. Others, like bundling up old newspapers or emptying the vacuum cleaner, were once-a-week chores.

Assigning jobs to children is one thing; getting them to perform without hassles or conflicts is quite another. Your success will depend largely upon your own attitude and approach to home duties. If a youngster can be given the impression that he is working with you and not for you, he will be more willing and cooperative.

"My daughter is always unhappy when I ask her to work in the kitchen with me," a neighbor complained of her nine-year-old. "She all but rebels."

We have noticed that this mother makes a practice of assigning the child dull routine jobs which she is trying to avoid herself, like wiping up spills or scouring a soiled sink. Sharing jobs that are both interesting and dull will teach a youngster that a certain degree of drudgery is present in almost every type of work effort.

Other mothers have problems with young kitchen helpers because they are not specific enough about duties to be performed. "Help me in the kitchen," is a request that can leave a youngster dangling. "I'll start the cake while you make the salad," is a more positive and direct approach.

While most parents will agree that giving children small jobs to do around the house is good training, they must also realize that children, like adults, need to feel that the tasks they are performing are necessary and helpful and not merely busy work routines.

Parents who decide to put their youngsters to work around the house are sooner or later confronted with the question of reward. Should a child be paid for what he does? The young child usually presents no problem in this respect. He is usually satisfied with "thank you for helping me" or "you did a good job." But as a youngster grows older, he develops a need for money and becomes aware that work and reward are related in our society.

After considering the various involvements that could develop, we decided that we would not pay our children for jobs from which they benefited equally with other members of the family. There are certain things that each of us *must* do in our daily routine. Paying a child for everything he does is likely to leave the impression that nothing is worth doing unless the effort is rewarded with money.

We found the best pattern was to give each youngster a small weekly allowance and then pay them for special jobs based on the family financial condition, which changed from time to time.

Mending socks and gloves, for example, were extra assignments for Lynn. Jim was always good around pets, so giving the dog a bath fell to his lot. We found, however, that most special jobs were of a seasonal nature. For Jim it was spring cleaning of the garage, which always seemed to accumulate a good deal of junk during the winter months. And in the fall, he was usually assigned the task of cleaning hand tools before they were put away for the winter.

Home chores can often create a rapport with your youngsters that can make your heart sing. One summer I was out of work for three months because of a back injury. Although I was on disability pay, we were pinching pennies to stay within our budget. I had not been thinking much about work around the house until that warm May morning Jim walked into my bedroom. He was ten at the time.

"Don't worry about the screens, Dad," he said. "I can do it, and you can give me my special pay when things get better."

The family that works together will cherish being together. ●

My Family, My Friends by Carol Amen

The jangling phone caught me arm-deep in scrub water. Only a few minutes remained before the first of my three children would come trooping in from school, and every housewife knows what hungry kids can do to a wet kitchen floor en route to the refrigerator.

After my hurried "Hello," a voice began explaining how I could help the handicapped of our county, a plea I could hardly interrupt—nor did the caller give me a chance. On and on he talked, giving the details. We would subscribe to a certain newspaper for three months, and he would donate half the subscription rate to the local handicapped. A rivulet of dirty water trickled down my arm and off my elbow to the floor.

Finally he paused for breath, and I explained politely that we already took the paper and preferred to make our charitable gifts direct. Despite the fact that he had invaded my privacy and inconvenienced me, I couldn't have been more courteous.

I had tackled the floor again by the time the first child arrived from school demanding to know what he could eat.

"Just a minute," I snapped. "Can't you see I'm busy? I'll fix your snack when I'm ready. Don't you know better than to pester me when I'm working?" I squirm even now, remembering.

Ever since then I've been pondering the difference in the way I treat strangers or guests and the manner in which I respond to my own family. Are others as guilty, I wondered, of exhibiting Amy Vanderbilt manners for outsiders while subjecting loved ones to repeated displays of short temper?

I searched for a way to change the situation. Perhaps I might occasionally pretend my family had come to visit me and were not permanent residents. Pressing them with service I might say, "Won't you have another biscuit, Bruce? It's so nice you could stop

121

your football game and come in and join us for dinner. Valerie, are the green beans done to your liking? I notice you're hiding a few in your napkin. Would you care for a bowser bag so you could take them home for later? Oh, you *are* home! I forgot. Jeff, could we drop you anywhere after dinner? No, I insist you not help with the dishes. Why, I'll just whisk them away and then later I can do them while you're all cozy watching TV. No, really, I don't mind. I *like* to wash dishes."

But I seriously doubt if that gambit would have prevailed more than a single night, even if I had tried it, because of its phoniness. Whatever else my faults with my kin, I tell myself righteously, at least I'm honest.

Then at the library I stumbled onto a book illustrating the ways of "manipulative" persons. Sometimes such people fail to communicate clearly the emotions they are experiencing, it said, or they communicate a different emotion from the one they are feeling.

For years, I realized, I had been playing "martyr" with my husband and children. While I'd always enjoyed being a wife and mother and had gotten a kick out of the less repetitious of the job's responsibilities, I forever expected my family to tell me what a great job I was doing.

I sought compliments on my banana cream pie and my occasionally waxed floors, and the fishing tactics I used were far from satisfactory. Either I waited pointedly for praise that was not forthcoming, or I nagged until I got someone to acknowledge that yes, the pie was more than just edible, it was delicious. Was I satisfied? No. I wanted to be appreciated!

Finally it struck me: Who was I to expect praise from my family when I so seldom gave it to them? Of course, I loved them and appreciated them, but did I tell them so, and in ways they could understand? Did I thank my husband for going to work every day, and the kids for doing well in school and staying out of trouble? I guess you know the answer. They always knew when I was grumpy, but they weren't as likely to find out when I was happy with them.

The family cat accompanied me as I wandered from room to room in the empty house, taking stock. I tried to visualize each of my children from the point of view of a strange mother, and I studied the characteristics of my absent husband as would an unattached female looking for a promising mate.

I peered into one son's room, and when I surveyed the neatness and order I realized with a pang that any parent would rejoice in a boy who rose daily and made his bed without being told, who was responsible without reminders for homework, lawn mowing, and music lessons. I had hardly acknowledged to myself the value of these traits, and I had certainly failed to convey appreciation to my son.

As I thought about it, I discovered individual qualities in each of my family—characteristics that I liked but seldom mentioned. All was not perfection. One son's room looked like a cyclone time in a garbage factory, but I found many things in his nature to be thankful for. Each was different, and as I thought of them separately from the others, I had different reactions.

I grabbed a notepad and pen and began the first in a series of love notes. "Thank you for trying so hard in school. Daddy and I know how many hours you have to work to keep up in math, and we appreciate your efforts. We love you." And, to another, "Thank you for being such a happy boy so much of the time. We appreciate your telling us about the plans and projects you are interested in. Thank you for doing your chores cheerfully. I love you."

To my husband: "Thank you for answering that first letter so long ago. I think we have a pretty good thing going, don't you? But I'm hoping we can make it even better. Thanks for your patience. I love you. PS: Thanks for going to work regularly, especially when you may not feel like it."

I placed the notes in strategic spots in each room and then had to wait until later in the day for them to be discovered. I was pretty impatient by the time the youngest and most skeptical asked, "How come you wrote me this note, Mom?"

I reinforced what the short letter had said, that I loved him and wanted to put down in writing my feelings of joy at having him for a son. Further, it didn't mean that I'd never again lose my temper with him. It just meant that as of this moment I was expressing my appreciation of him as a person, unique and important to the family scheme of things.

Not much happened that first night. There was no miraculous transformation in which the family suddenly appreciated me, but I reminded myself that that wasn't the purpose. I was trying to appreciate *them*, with no strings attached.

From then on I tried to find at least one instance each day in which I could express individual appreciation or praise. Sometimes it was hard to think of anything noteworthy, but I didn't mind how far I had to reach for a positive statement. "Thank you for remembering to clean the ring out of the bathtub" did not seem a ridiculous remark if it was true.

After about a week and a half of my impromptu notewriting, as we were clearing the table one evening, my least communicative child approached me. "That was sure a good dinner, Mom," he said with what I judged to be real sincerity in his voice. Earlier I might have quipped, "It's about time somebody said so," or "I don't believe it." Instead I said simply, "Thank you for telling me."

I don't suppose I'll continue this system indefinitely. The notes are already shorter and the span between them longer. But I'm looking around for other ways to keep from slipping in the taking-them-for-granted rut, little recognitions that I realize how fortunate I am to have them, just as they are.

Why shouldn't I treat my family like company? After all, they are very special! ●

The Weapons of Wives by Ruth Bell Graham

Anyone who has even a nodding acquaintance with the Westminster Catechism knows that man's chief end is to glorify God and to enjoy him forever. Psalm 37:4 tells us that we are to delight ourselves in the Lord. The Septuagint translation has the most marvelous rendering of these words. It says, "Indulge thyself with delight in the Lord." Do you indulge yourself in the Lord? Do you enjoy the peace of sins forgiven? Do you enjoy sharing Jesus Christ with others?

Someone has said that the best way to get a child to eat is to let him see his parents enjoying their food. It doesn't make a great deal of difference how much you believe if you aren't "behaving." I have a friend who is as orthodox as they come, but she is such a chronic worrier that her six children fail to see the resemblance between the God she claims to follow and the God she expresses through her life.

I recall a night some years ago when I got up with one or another of the children about five times before morning. Bill wasn't home. When it came time to waken the household, we were all sleepy. I picked the baby out of bed and didn't bother to change him, just dumped him in his high chair. I grabbed the first bathrobe I could find; my hair was a mess, my face was a mess. At the breakfast table, every time Gigi, our eldest, would start to say something, Bunny, the youngest daughter, would interrupt her. Finally Gigi banged down her fork, pushed back her chair, and said, "Mother, between looking at you and listening to Bunny and smelling the baby, I'm just not hungry!"

Are you taking away someone's appetite for Christ? The best definition of a saint that I ever heard is, "A saint is one who makes it easy to believe in Jesus." Are you making it easy for those about you to believe in him?

Wives, what about your attitude toward your husbands? You will remember that when God created woman, he created her a help, meet for her husband. We so often print the word "helpmeet," but that's not what the Bible says. She is to be a help, meet for her husband; that means a help suited for her husband. The New Testament says that wives are to "adapt" themselves to their husbands.

Each man needs something a little bit different from what another man may need. Are you trying to adapt yourself to your husband and be the kind of wife *he* needs—not the kind you think he needs, but the kind he really needs? Are you trying to please him? If we want to please someone, we must please him in his own way. Stop and ask yourself, "If I were a man, what sort of wife would I want to come home to?" Are you that kind of wife? If not, then become that kind of wife!

The best advice I ever heard given to a woman whose husband was not a Christian was: "Your business is not to make him good but to make him happy!" It's God's business to make him good. You take care of the possible and trust God for the impossible.

A wife has two God-given weapons: love—this includes ministering to your husband's immediate needs; and prayer—keep your mouth shut and pray. We are to keep busy in our department and stay out of God's. We are to take care of the possible and let God take care of the impossible.

I heard a true story about a mother of five children. She had a militantly unbelieving husband, who took great delight in criticizing his wife, making fun of her faith in front of the children, and telling her faults before guests. He did everything he could to undermine what she was trying to do. And yet those five children grew up to be dedicated Christian men and women.

Late in her life a friend who knew of the difficult situation asked the mother how she had managed to cope with it. She replied, "I made it a point never to argue with my husband and never to criticize him; and I made it a point never to miss the opportunity, when I tucked the children in at night, to read to them from the Word of God and to pray with them."

What is your attitude toward your children? Do you consider them a trust from God, eternal souls for whom Christ died?

Did you ever hear God say to you, as Pharaoh's daughter did to Moses' mother, "Take this child . . . and nurse it for me, and I will give thee thy wages"?

Did you ever find your own heart praying John 17:24, "Father, I will that they also, whom thou hast given me, be with me where I am"?

As the writer John Trapp said in the 17th century, "A child's mind is like a small-necked bottle. If you pour in the wine too rapidly, much of it spills over and is lost." Teach them early to know the Lord, to trust him, to confess their sins to him. Teach them early to put their faith in God.

Salvation is a miracle of grace, but if you do your part, God will do his. Teach your children that God loves them and is beside them always. Teach them to love and trust his will however hard it may be. Teach them not just to *say* their prayers, but to *pray*—to talk with God, to know that God is interested in everything they have to say. Every animal about our place—dogs, cats, canaries—has been prayed for many, many times. Teach the children that God cares about everything that concerns them.

I was blessed by being reared in a missionary's home in China. My father was a medical missionary; he was head of the surgical department of the mission hospital and Mother helped in the women's clinic. I grew up watching their concern for other people. Daddy was a good doctor. Yet he felt that that mission hospital existed primarily to tell people about Jesus Christ. I saw their concern for our family. And they didn't know that these and other things made a deep impression on me. I never got up in the morning, for instance, but what I saw Daddy reading his Bible. I never went to tell him goodnight at bedtime without finding him down on his knees, praying. Mother might not have time to read her Bible in the mornings—she was getting breakfast—but she always read her Bible in bed at night.

One final word: Are you one of those who is so weighed down by your sins that you feel it's quite hopeless? You are the sort of person God loves.

A mother of 13 children was asked which one she loved the most. She replied, "The one that is sick until he's well, and the one that is lost until he's found."

God has been missing you, loving you, searching for you. I don't know the burdens you are carrying, but he does. This business of raising a family, with all its problems, is a difficult job.

Give your burdens to him; he'll take them. All he asks is that you love him and live with him. ●